KP

TO
ORLANDO
&
WALT DISNEY WORLD®

Look out for other great titles in
the Knapsack Guide Series

KNAPSACK GUIDE TO DISNEYLAND® RESORT PARIS

KNAPSACK GUIDE TO BARCELONA & PORTAVENTURA®

KNAPSACK GUIDE TO LONDON

KNAPSACK GUIDE TO BRIGHTON & HOVE

Get your hands on them and start planning
some more exciting trips!

Where do you think we should do next?
Been somewhere interesting?
Let us know!
hello@knapsackguides.com

KNAPSACK GUIDE
TO
ORLANDO
&
WALT DISNEY WORLD®

essential guides for streetwise kids

Written and Researched
by
Michael and Helenor Rogers

Illustrations by Laura Broad

www.knapsackguides.com

Knapsack Guide to Orlando & Walt Disney World®

Acknowledgements

Dedicated to everyone who helped us along the way; with enormous thanks. Especially to our proof readers Joanne Gray, Susie Coyle.

A big thanks to Funway Holidays for a top trip to Florida to research this book. We were well and truely looked after. Ta very much. Also a huge hug to all the lovely people at Disney.

We proudly present the fourth ever Knapsack Guide.

First published in 2005. Hurrah!
Fashioned with passion by Helenor and Michael Rogers. Funky drawings and cartoons by Laura Broad.

Photographs kindly supplied by the Walt Disney Company Ltd. © Disney and by Universal Orlando©. Don't they look good?!

Proudly Published by Knapsack Publishing Ltd.

Knapsack Publishing Ltd
The Beach Hut
PO Box 124
Hove
BN3 3UY

© Knapsack Publishing Ltd 2005.

Printed by the kind people at Gutenberg Press Ltd.

ISBN: 0-9545212-4-2

CONTENTS

INTRODUCTION

How excited are you about going to Walt Disney World® (WDW) Resort? A whole lot probably, and you jolly well should be 'cos it is going to be the best holiday in your entire life, ever. Honest!

Loads of kids only dream of visiting the Magic Kingdom, and you are going - wow! It truly is fantastic; from the super exhilarating rides, the spectacular shows, the loveable characters and the tempting shops; just so much to ensure you enjoy yourself to the max.

CAN YOU HANDLE IT?

Some of you thrill seekers might think you are too old for Disney® but don't be too hasty, it's not just for babies you know. In fact it can be a bit annoying if you are little 'cos you might not get to go on all of the rides. The resorts in Florida are fun factories for people of all ages, except boring, cissy, scaredy cats. They are especially exciting for up for it adventure junkies - is that you?

What kind of car does Mickey Mouse's wife drive? A minnie !

Not only do the Disney® delights await you - don't miss out on the spectacles at Universal Studios Florida® or the heart pumping rides at Universal's Island of Adventure®. The Orlando area is kid heaven, bet you're getting really excited now!!!

About This Guide

There are loads of books out there about WDW (we'll call it that from now on) but hardly any just for kids themselves. Hard to believe, eh? Like you're not the ones that the place was built for in the first place or anything! Well we thought we should do something

THE UNMISSABLE...

about it and fill you in on the crucial info that every kids needs to know - here it is...

Knapsack Guide to Walt Disney World® Resort

The aim of this guide book is to tell you what you need to know, not what grown ups, the parks, or the holiday brochures think you should know. It includes all the vital knowledge along with a few fun facts and side splitting jokes (we think so anyway!). If lace making and matchstick modelling are more your thing just stop reading now, you probably won't enjoy this book or WDW - too way out for you man!

The Layout

The layout is simple and easy to use. Information is split into 5 main sections:

The Essentials

Takes you through the basic things you need to think about to get the most out of your trip including the best way to get there, how to get around when you are there and importantly, where to find good loos.

The Facts

Gives you a fascinating low down on how the magic of Disney® came about. There is also crucial stuff you didn't even know you needed to know about the park itself, factastic!

Hanging Out

The crucial info. on where it's at and where it's not. There is such a lot to do at WDW and in Orlando, different things that appeal to different kinds of kids - make sure you go to the places that will thrill your pants off.

The Ultimate

If you just can't be bothered to read all the detail (you'll be missing out...) then head for here, the best the parks have to offer jammed into a day.

Handy Stuff

Does exactly what it says and pulls together useful details such as websites with Disney® info, cash point locations and where to send postcards home.

Who is the blue guy?

Scout is the knapsack guide. He knows millions of useful and useless facts and figures and will help you make the most of your holiday of a lifetime. You can find out more about Scout at 💻 www.knapsackguides.com.

Think You Know More Than Scout?

Fancy yourself as a bit of a travel guide? Then maybe you can help us out. We are always looking for kids to help Scout by telling us the latest stuff. All contributors will get a name check in the next book so if you've got something to say get in touch. Contact us on hello@knapsackguides.com.

What do you get if you cross a Martian with a golf score? A little green bogey!

About 💻 www.knapsackguides.com

Don't forget to visit 💻 www.knapsackguides.com for all of the latest info. on WDW. There are also loads of photos, latest timings for the big events and links to useful websites. You can also write to us or post notices so that other knapsackers can see your views – get surfing!!

Warning!

We do try very, very hard at Knapsack Publishing to get things right, but sometimes we make mistakes and other times things change. We can't all be perfect! So if you find something that's not right please tell us about it. Again contact us by email on hello@knapsackguides.com.

Planning Your Activities

Planning might sound like a dull chore but it isn't, honest! It's when you get to find out about all of the exciting things that await you in Orlando, when you get so excited about going that you dream about it every single night (and every day during boring things

PLANNING PRANKS

Planning is a great way to make sure you get to do what you want to do and not the boring bits that dullards dream of – but you need to have a few pranks up your sleeve.

- Do a survey of what everyone wants to do, and then announce the results. But sneakily miss out the things you don't fancy doing and make sure all of your 'must do's, are at the top of the list.
- Suggest everyone has a job to do to prepare for the holiday. Things like organising a First Aid Kit, sorting out the suntan lotion, preparing the luggage – you kindly volunteer to do all the planning (making sure you do all the things you want..!).
- Say you have done a comprehensive review of all of the best bits in Florida using guide books and the internet and have come up with the best things to do (which just happen to be your faves).

    That should do it!

Teacher: I do wish you'd pay a little attention in assembly...
Pupil: I'm paying as little attention as I can, sir..!

like the 'News' or school assembly) and sort out the bits you know you want to do from the bits that you'll avoid at all costs. It's really worth it, there is so much to do you won't be able to pack it in (unless you go for a whole year or more) and you want to make sure you don't miss out the unmissable, don't you?!

What to Read

This book is a good place to start (you've probably worked that out already!) but don't read the whole book cover to cover, dip in and out of the bits you want to read - it's not a story book! If you just want to know what is there for you to do, go straight to the 'Hanging Out' sections. If you would like an idea of a great day out in each of the main parks then head on to 'The Ultimate' and decide on what you fancy doing.

Day Planner			
	What?	Where?	Notes
Morning			
LUNCH			
Afternoon			
DINNER / REST			
Evening			

The Day Planners

In 'The Ultimate' we have used a Day Planner (see above) to show what to do on the best day ever. Print out extra blank copies of this at ⌨ www.knapsack-guides.com.

You'll need to be flexible as event times change and there will probably be queues or even some places may be closed, but it'll give you a start point.

Web Wandering

You can't beat the web for fact finding and WDW is a popular topic 'cos people love it so much. That means there are hundreds of sites (some of which are really rubbish!) so be warned! There is fab info. on ⌨www.knapsackguides.com and on the official sites ⌨www.waltdisneyworld.com (you have to register here but it is worth it...) and at ⌨www.universalorlando.com. Other sites are in Handy Stuff later...

Things to Pack

You know you need to take all the obvious things like clothes, trainers, a hat (for those bad hair days), your swimmers etc; but there are also a few other handy bits to pack :

TIP TOP ITEMS TO PACK...

- Money – as much as poss, change it into dollars
- Camera – to send us your top pics
- Fanny pack (!) – as they say in the US, a bum bag to us, handy to keep your bits in one piece when you are on the rides
- Strap on sandals that won't fall off on the rides
- Chargers / spare batteries to keep the gadgets going
- A fantastic guidebook (now where can you find one of those...?)

In terms of essential hand luggage pack:

- A walkman / MP3 player / Gameboy / games / playing cards – to listen to tunes by the pool and pass the time away in boring air-ports, pack near the top to get your mits on them easily
- Food and Drink – Sucking sweets, chewy mints, crisps, some fruit (apple, satsumas, banana), nuts, still water (fizzy is a bit windy). Not choc, it can get really messy...
- Reading Material – Comics, magazines, puzzle books and a story book are must takes, you'll have lots of reading time. Pack this book near the top for quick reference.
- Emergency Rations – Toothbrush, hairbrush, teddy (at the bottom, nobody will know), spare pair of knickers, cap, sunnies, shorts; just in case your bag gets lost on the way over!

Now you're sorted!

What you can get there...

You can buy anything in WDW and Orlando, in fact some sado's go to Orlando just to shop! There are bargains to be had and some super cool shops (including the best VANS shop ever). More later...

Planning For The Journey

It's a long, long way to the land of fun; the aeroplane ride itself will be a minimum of 9 hours and there is a long, dull, dull, dull transfer at the end. It can be real-llllly boring if you haven't prepared for it, honest.

- It is 4328 miles (6964 km) to Orlando from London.
- The flight takes at least 9 hours - but it looks like only 4 as the time is 5 hours behind UK time.

You'll see loads of bored stroppy kids sitting on the airport floor - you'd never believe they were on the holiday of a lifetime! On the other hand it can be reallllly exciting if you make the journey part of the best-holiday-ever experience, with a bit of preparation. Pack a rucksack to take on the 'plane with journey essentials.

Getting There / Staying There

The only way to get to Orlando is to go by aeroplane, an adventure in itself.

You might be going as independent travellers (especially if the grown ups are web gurus) or you could be on a package deal. Package deal companies and airlines sometimes provide extra special offers for kids - make sure you get your treats!

ANNOYING QUESTIONS TO ASK WHEN IN AN AEROPLANE...

- Can you explain the aerodynamics of this plane in comparison to a Harrier Jump Jet? (to the Air Steward)
- Can I go to the loo? (Just as the air steward has put the meal down in front of you)
- Where does the wee in the loo disappear to?
- Does that large man have to pay for two seats?
- Did you hear that noise, has something fallen off? (Every 5 mins)
- My window is frosting up - could you nip outside and de-ice it?

What do you call a flock of birds who fly in formation?
The red sparrows!

THE ESSENTIALS

13

TREATS FOR KIDS

Here are some of the current in-flight treats on offer for Orlando bound kids, these change all the time so check out the brochures and web for the latest deals...

- Virgin - Backpack of goodies, seat back TV, shows kids own channel with blockbuster movies <u>and</u> Nintendo video games (on most flights). Kids grub too, order in advance.
- British Airways - Shoulder Bag of goodies (inc. Top Trumps), seat back TV with Kids Toons, Tunes & Films, priority boarding and 'feed kids first policy' with special kids menu. Book in advance.
- Funway Holidays - Fab flight treats from the airlines above, plus free kids meals and kids clubs in some resorts.
- Thomson - 'Kid Zone' designed by kids for kids provides your own TV and radio stations, back pack with games, pocket money priced gifts and kid's meals (extra cost).
- Unijet / First Choice - Kids pack, 3 movies, music, kids food (extra cost), free ice cream. Free kids meals in some resorts.
- Thomas Cook - BYO goodies!!

Orlando International Airport

- 1 Airport Boulevard, Orlando
- ☎ +1 407 825 2001
- 🖳 www.orlandoairports.net

Virgin, Continental and British Airways fly into Orlando, this airport is a bit of a nightmare so be prepared! It is the 24th biggest airport in the world and so has lots to do, but it takes a while to get around.

Apparently it is one of airports best liked by travellers, some say it is the best in the US - they must be very patient. Not only do you have the boring US immigration to deal with (where they check your passport and take your thumb print) but you have to pick up your suitcase only to give it away again and then pick it up again after a train ride and a walk through the airport. It feels never ending! Then you might have to wait ages to pick up a hire car, make sure you've got some reading left or a game to keep you amused...

What pie can fly?
A magpie.

Orlando Sanford Airport

Cleveland Blvd., Sanford, Florida

☎ +1 407 585 4000

🖥 www.orlandosanfordairport.com

DID YOU KNOW?

That August is the busies month at Sanfod airport with over 70,000 international flights arriving.

Most of the charter holidays fly into Orlando Sanford Airport, a bit of a smaller and easier option allowing you to get out into the fun much quicker. Even though it's small it still has an arcade, a few shops and a food court. For an additional charge ($10 kids, $20 adults) you can go into the swanky 'Guest House' where you get free drinks and snacks, latest films on a huge telly and best of all you can play on one of the 8 Sony PS2's. Well worth it!

JET LAG CURES

Lots of peeps, especially grown ups suffer from jet lag, when they get really tired and a bit dizzy after travelling across time zones. Try these cures:

- Set your watch to the time at your holiday place as soon as you get on the aeroplane, try to act as you normally would at this time.
- Light tricks - get as much daylight during the new day time and wear sunnies / an eye mask when it is your new night-time.
- Water - drink as much as you can and spray it on your face to keep awake during new daytime hours, no water fights though!
- Put brown paper bags on your feet for the journey.

Places to Stay

OK, so you may not have much say about where you stay, but here is some info. and advice so that you can have an opinion about it nevertheless!

WDW® Resort Hotels

So what is so good about staying at WDW? The theming of the hotels is really cool, the imagineers have gone totally wild in some! The Pop

DID YOU KNOW?

It would take more than 20m cans of Coke to fill one of the Coke cups at the Home-Run Hotel in the All-Star Sports Resort!

THE ESSENTIALS

- **All Star Resorts *** (Animal Kingdom)**
  3 resorts with 3 themes, sport, movies or music shown by massive icons - like a huge Pongo, surf board and a giant drum kit. Really bright and colourful with 2 fab heated pools. Pizza delivery service, cool when you are too tired to move in the evenings.

- **Animal Kingdom Lodge***** (Animal Kingdom)**
  Can you imagine having zebras in your back garden? You get pretty close to it here as they wander in the park surrounding the hotel along with giraffes, deer and pretty birds. Nice pool but not huge. Don't forget your binoculars.

- **Pop Century Resort*** (MGM Studios)**
  V. similar to All Stars except with a 20th Century theme. Climb up the stairs hidden in yoyo's and play on the giant size table football court or in the flower power pool. Pizza delivery too!

- **Wilderness Lodge and Villas*** (Magic Kingdom)**
  Take a walk on the wild side when you stay here. The hot spring / waterfall pool is fantastic and the wilderness theming top notch. You get to take the boat launch to the Magic Kingdom, coo-el.

- **Polynesian*** (Magic Kingdom)**
  It's a totally tropical island theme down here with your own beach and erupting volcano pool with water slide. You can hire canoes to paddle around the lake and amuse yourself in the games room. Fab dinner show with flaming torches and character breakfasts.

- **Caribbean Beach Resort** (Epcot)**
  It's pool-tastic here! Six brightly coloured villages named after Caribbean islands, each have their own pool as well as the huge main pool with waterfall and slides. Also has a games room, boating on the lake and the popular food court and pizza delivery!

- **Port Orleans Resorts*** (Downtown Disney)**
  There are 2 resorts here, the Riverside (used to be called Dixie Landings) and the French Quarter. Both are themed in good 'ole southern USA style, big mansions and beautiful gardens. Groovy pools (watch out for the alligators!) and you can use all the amenities in both places. Chill out with a bit of fishing,

DID YOU KNOW?

There are so many hotel rooms in WDW you could stay in a different one every night for the next 55 years!

Century Resort and All Star Resorts are good examples of this with stair cases hidden in huge skittles and wardrobes that look like gym lockers! At the Polynesian you are

WHY STAY AT WDW?

- Extra Magic Hour - Each park allows WDW hotel guests to enter one hour early (or stay in longer) at least one day per week. It's worth planning your days to take advantage of this.

- Transportation - Full and unlimited use of the monorail, buses and boats of the WDW transporation system. You can also use 'Disney's Magical Express service' which gives free transportation to and from Orlando airport.*

- 'Chargecard' - You can spend what you like on your resort ID card and pay at the end of your trip. This means the adults are a bit easier with the readies, they don't realise how much they are spending!

- Shopping Drop Off - You can shop 'til you drop without lugging bags around, they will magically be transported right back to your hotel room.

- Free Parking at the parks.

- Meet Disney®Characters at hotels.

- Mickey Mouse soaps and shampoos in the rooms.

- Use of the other WDW resort hotel facilities, their guests get first dabs but if there is space you can for example check out the wildlife the Animal Kingdom hotel.

* Limited offer, may be retracted at any time...

greeted with an 'Aloha' and zebras and giraffes roam in the gardens of the Animal Kingdom Lodge. Staying at a WDW resort hotel really is living the Disney® experience. Highly recommended.

Unfortunately we don't have enough space to cover off all of the WDW hotels, we've just included those that are especially kid-cool. You will have a good time wherever you rest your weary head!

Other Hotels

There is a big chance you might be staying in one of the hundreds of other hotels in the Orlando area. The benefit of these are that you do get to escape the Disney® drama and have a chance to experience another side to Orlando and see other parks, attractions (and bargain shops if you are a mad shopaholic!).

You will probably be in one of three areas:

Disney Hotel Plaza

These hotels are right on the doorstep of Downtown Disney and are almost WDW resort hotels except they are not owned by Disney! The Hilton even gives you the Extra Magic Hour benefit and the Grosvenor Resort has character breakfasts, usually only for WDW hotels. Doubletree Guest Suites know who are important, they have a special kid's own check in area as well as a pool, cinema, games room and video arcade.

Lake Buena Vista
🖥 www.kidsuites.com.net

Just 10 mins from the parks with loads of places to eat and shop. The coolest place on the block is the Holiday Inn Sunspree Resort who say 'Kids are Kings' (who are we to argue?), with kids

What
is a kings favourite weather?
Reign!!

How does a king know how tall he is?
He uses his ruler!!

check in and unique 'Kidsuites'; your own room within the family room that has a TV, Nintendo, CD player, clock radio, fun phone and bunk beds. Great for a bit of privacy when you need a break! Other Holiday Inns in the Orlando area have similar kid-first facilities.

International Drive
🖥 www.internationaldriveorlando.com

A really popular location with loads of hotels, every restaurant chain, themed attractions (Skull Kingdom, Sky Venture!) and of course lots of shops. Also close

WHY SURVIVE I-DRIVE ?

- You can eat a burger in the world's largest McDonald's, there is also 24 hour dining and more than 150 restaurants!
- It is where you'll find the world's only upside down three-storey building (WonderWorks).
- You can shop till you drop
- You can sky dive in a wind tunnel (Sky Venture), Walk under a waterfall (Pirates Cove Adventure Golf) and touch an iceberg (Titanic Exhibition)
- There are live alligators (Congo River Golf & Exploration Company), you can swim with dolphins (Discovery Cove) or touch a stingray (Sea World).

Never a dull moment!

to Wet 'n Wild and Universal Orlando® and downtown Orlando itself. It's full of holidaying Brits - it's sometimes hard to believe you're in Florida! An impressive looking hotel is the Doubletree Castle Hotel, it is supposed to look a bit like Cinderella's castle in the Magic Kingdom, not sure if it quite makes it, but impressive nevertheless.

GET LOST!

It's possible that you'll get lost in the parks or at your hotel - but don't worry... pretend it's a bit of an adventure:

- Ask one of the cast members for help... they wear an "I" on their costumes and will happily help you out or answer any questions!
- Give your parents a photo of yourself, so that if you do get lost they can show people what you look like.
- Agree an emergency rendezvous spot with the others you are with - for example, if someone is missing everyone makes their way to Casey's Corner on Main Street USA®. Don't pick the obvious place like Cinderella's castle - everyone meets there.
- Look out for signs on one of the rides / attractions and then locate this on your map. Use this to trace your way to the agreed meeting point.
- Think about taking Walkie Talkies with you. They are quite cheap nowadays (esp. in the USA, less than $10) and are great fun as well as being useful.

Why did the chewing gum cross the road?
It was stuck to the leg of a chicken !!!

T H E   E S S E N T I A L S

19

Getting Around

Let the grown ups take the strain organising getting to and from the parks. You'll probably go by hire car, use the WDW monorail, ferries or the resort shuttle bus - not particularly exciting.

Just make sure you are up bright and early to get on all of the biggies without a huge queue and take advantage of the 'extra magic hours' if you are a WDW resident.

I NEED A WEE

Sometimes you just have to go - now! Luckily the loos in the parks are generally clean, they are on the maps and are easy to find! There can be quite long queues during the summer when it gets busy, so go whenever you have the opportunity!

Also remember that WDW is huge and you probably will get lost getting around... This can make the hire car option a bit stressful at times, be prepared for dodgy navigation and stroppy drivers, there will be arguements... Worth taking your head-phones and tuning in to some groovy tunes!

Maps

You can pick up maps galore in Orlando - at the airport, every ticket shop, shopping mall and at hotels. They are handy for finding your way around, definitely pick some up.

There is a map of the whole of WDW and Universal Resort Orlando in "Hanging Out". However make sure you get a map from each of the park entrances as you come through the gates, they include show times and any special events too. Ask at guest services if they have run out.

Getting Around the Parks

Unless you are in a buggy (and then you are probably not able to read) then you are likely to be getting around the parks under your own steam by walking! Walking is the best way to get from place to place, you get to take in the magical surroundings as you pass from place to place. Just make sure you wear a comfortable pair of trainers or strapped-on sandals, you don't want them falling off half way up a roller coaster, do you?!

Useful Info

Tickets / Passports

www.waltdisneyworld.com
ⓘ Costs: get the oldies to check these out.

If you've not bought a package deal then you need to think about what kind of ticket you'll need, best to do it before you go!

Remember Disney® classify kids as under 10's - so you 10+'s are mini adults! Certainly means you'll pay the adult price 'though doesn't mean you can drive or vote...pity.

You can buy premium tickets and ultimate tickets (only available to UK customers who book in advance), depending on the length of your stay or how rich you are!! Premium tickets are valid for

TICKET INTEL.

- 1 day tickets - access to one of the 4 main parks only.
- 5/7 Day Premium Tickets - access to the 4 main parks plus 3/5 visits to ANY of the other Disney parks including the water parks, sports complex and the excellent Disneyquest Indoor Interactive Theme Park. You can visit more than 1 main park each day and tickets are valid for 14 days from the first day of use.
- 14/21 Day Ultimate Tickets - access to ANY of the Disney parks including the main parks, water parks, sports complex and the excellent Disneyquest Indoor Interactive Theme Park. You can visit more than place each day and tickets are valid for 14/21 days from the first day of use.

either 5 or 7 days whilst Ultimate tickets are for 14 or 21 days. Each have their own rules and regulations so you need to understand what you can do!

You can also buy 1 day 'Magic Your Way' base tickets from the park gates, which grants you access to that park. You can pay an extra fee to upgrade this on a per day basis, as they say 'the longer you play the less you pay'.

How can you double your money?
Look at it in a mirror.

Queue Jumping

Yes, you can do this without everyone going mad at you! Fastpass is a great Disney® invention, the quick way to queue. Check out what rides offer this and go to your favourite first. Look above the machine to check the ride time - make sure you aren't doing

MUST-DO FASTPASS PLACES

Mission: Space	EPCOT
Test Track	EPCOT
Kilimanjaro Safaris	Animal Kingdom
DINOSAUR	Animal Kingdom
Kali River Rapids	Animal Kingdom
It's Tough to be a Bug!	Animal Kingdom
Rock 'n' Roller Coaster	MGM Studios
Tower of Terror	MGM Studios
Star Tours	MGM Studios
Indiana Jones Epic Stunt Spectacular!	MGM Studios
Splash Mountain	Magic Kingdom
Space Mountain	Magic Kingdom
Stitch's Great Escape	Magic Kingdom
The Haunted Mansion	Magic Kingdom
Buzz Lightyear's Space Ranger Spin	Magic Kingdom
Big Thunder Mountain Railroad	Magic Kingdom

anything else then! If it is OK then stick in your park pass and get a Fastpass with your alloted time on it. Then just return to the ride in your time slot and get into the shorter Fastpass queue - delightful!

NOTE: if you can't save more than 30 mins with the FASTPASS then don't bother, it's quicker to queue.

When you get a Fastpass the ticket tells you when you can get your next one, make a plan to take advantage of this. Get as many as you can before 1pm, (Mission: Space and Test Track by 11am) they often run out after then or have ridiculous waiting times - up to 7 hours!!!

Opening Hours

http://disneyworld.disney.go.com/wdw/calendar/parkhours

The parks are open 365 days a year – even Christmas Day, the busiest day in the Magic Kingdom. The opening hours vary throughout the year, best check to find out the precise hours for when you are there.

As a general rule they open at 9am, closing from 6-8pm, with Animal Kingdom closing first. During the summer the Magic Kingdom can stay open as late as 1am with EPCOT and MGM open until 9 or 10pm.

When To Visit

As you would expect the busy times are when you guys (and when US kids) are on school holiday and when the sun shines. This basically means the sunny

PUBLIC HOLIDAYS

The parks do get busier during the US Public Holidays - and there are lots of them! Days to avoid unless you like the crowds are:

- Christmas - New Year: 18 December-2nd January
- Martin Luther King Day: Third Monday in January
- President's Day: Third Monday in February
- Easter (date varies): March / April
- Memorial Day: Last Monday in May
- Independence Day: 4th July
- Labor Day: First Monday in September
- Columbus Day: Second Monday in October
- Veterans Day: November 11th
- Thanksgiving: Fourth Thursday of November

23

but quieter times are April to May (avoiding Easter) and early September to late October.

Avoid public holidays - it's sooooo busy then!

What's On When...

Whenever you go to WDW there will be lots to do, but there are some extra special events that happen

Month	Events	Rating
January	New Year Celebration WDW Marathon, 20,000 running 26.2 miles around all 4 major parks	☺☺☺☺ ☺☺☺
Feb.	Atlanta Braves at Disney's Wide World of Sports complex for spring training.	☺☺☺
Apr- Jun	Epcot International Flower & Garden Festival with 30 million colorful blooms and interactive garden activities	☺☺
July	July 4th Celebrations - Spectacular displays throughout the WDW Resort.	☺☺☺☺
Oct.	Mickey's Not-So-Scary Halloween Party fright-fest in the Magic Kingdom featuring a kid's parade, trick-or-treating throughout the park, face painting and more	☺☺☺☺☺
Nov.	Holidays Around the World celebration at Epcot, sharing delightful holiday traditions from all around the globe.	☺☺☺☺
Dec.	Light spectaculars, fantasy parades, unforgettable parties - they know how to do Christmas here!	☺☺☺☺☺

around the same time every year. Check www.knapsackguides.com for actual dates. Five smile events above are best (duh!).

The Weather

Weather by time of year

The table on the next page shows the weather you can expect in Florida, but be prepared. If you are (un)lucky it could be hurricane season and you may have to hunker down for a couple of days. Generally it is pretty warm, much warmer than the UK. Precipitation is just a fancy word for 'wet stuff'; rain or

	J	F	M	A	M	J	J	A	S	O	N	D
Avg. Max (°C)	22	23	26	28	31	33	33	33	32	29	26	23
Avg. Min (°C)	9	10	13	15	19	22	23	23	22	18	14	11
Precipitation	58	76	81	46	91	185	183	173	152	61	58	56

snow to you and me. It is quite damp in Florida (humid and stormy in the Summer, drizzly in Winter), in between times are best, in Spring and Autumn.

Dosh

The money (currency), in Florida is the US dollar ($). Each dollar is made up of 100 cents (c). Notes are in $1, $2, $5, $10, $20, $50 and $100 denominations. Coins are 25-cent, 10-cent, 5-cent, and 1-cent pieces, usually known as a quarter, dime, nickel, and a penny.

If you want to know what your spending money is worth you need to check the exchange rate, e.g. currently £1 is equal to $1.87, so £20 is $37.40.

Time to.....

The time in Florida is GMT -5 hours, five hours behind the UK. So 10am in Orlando is 3pm in London.

Tipping...

People are very generous in the US, they like to leave a tip to say thank you for good service. Now we don't mean a tip like 'smile like you mean it next time', we mean a bit of wad. We know it might be hard, parting with your hard earned cash, but it is the done thing here. A dollar will usually do.

Phrasebook

You might think that going to the US will be easy from a language point of view - they speak English there don't they? Well they do... but not all of the words are

Handy Translations

US	UK	US	UK
Restroom	Toilet	Candy	Sweets
Bill	Note (money)	Check	Bill
Chips	Crisps	French Fries	Chips
Sub	Bread Roll	Subway	Underground
Trunk	Car Boot	Hood	Car Bonnet
Cookie	Biscuit	Biscuit	Salty scone
Sidewalk	Pavement	Pavement	Road
Crib	Cot	Cot	Fold up Bed
Fanny	Bottie (your)	Gas	Petrol
Shorts	Pants	Pants	Trousers
Sneakers	Trainers	Vest	Waistcoat

the same as the ones we use! Watch out if you walk on the pavement or if you say you're going out in your shorts!

Accidents and Emergencies

Hopefully you won't need to know this bit; but just in case. If you have an accident and need an emergency repair job done go to the First Aid point, there is one in every park, generally not far from the entrance. Ask a Cast Member for help or directions.

Disney have fully trained nursing staff who will tend to your every need and help you out.

MEDICAL EMERGENCY

In case of a real medical emergency or serious accident or if you need the Police or Fire Brigade telephone ☎911 (9,911 from your hotel room) and clearly ask for help.

Take a deep breath and tell the person on the end of the line:

- Your name
- Where you are
- Details about the problem

Speak slowly. Stay on the line until the person tells you to hang up. It is very important that you only do this in an emergency, if you cause a false alarm you might stop the emergency services going to a real accident and someone else might die. You will get into big trouble so be warned!

Special Needs

🖥 www.waltdisneyworld.com [Guests with Disabilities, at bottom of page]
☎ WDW +1 407 939 7807 (TTY: +1 407 939 7670)
🖥 www.universalorlando.co.uk [Select Guest Services, then ADA]
☎ Universal +1 407 363 8000

Don't let having special needs spoil your fun! From height adjusted water fountains, allergy-friendly chefs, video, handheld and reflective captioning for the hearing impaired, companion loos, braille guide books and much more - Orlando is for all.

Getting the Info.

Unfortunately we don't have masses of space to include all of the info. for kids with special needs, much as we'd like to - sorry! So we've just got the vital stuff.

WEE!

We all need to go sometime! Luckily most of the loos in the parks have wheelchair-friendly cubicles and some have other special cubicles if you need extra help.

Both Disney® and Universal make a real effort to ensure the parks can be enjoyed by absolutely anybody and absolutely everybody. Each produce a guide for disabled guests that can be accessed via their websites, ordered by 'phone or picked up from Guest Services at the main parks.

Staying There

The WDW Hotels really cater well for every guest whatever they need. From ramps to braille pad signs, TTY phones to strobe smoke detectors and closed-captioned televisions in specially adapted rooms. Just make sure you let the hotels know what you need they will make every effort to help.

When you arrive...

Go to the Guest Relations desk where you can discuss any help you will need. The staff there can answer questions, give you advice or provide special help and

SPECIAL PASSES

WDW Guest Relations issue 'Guest Assistance Cards' to last all of your holiday. This allows cast members to do things like let you wait in a shaded area, sit at the front in the theatres, or letting you in to attractions through secret entrances. They are quite strict about it and tell everyone that they are not for skipping queues, just to ensure those with special needs have a wonderful time!

can sort you out with a 'Guest Assistance Card' if you are very lucky!

Getting around...

Special parking areas for guests with disabilities are available throughout WDW, but you need a valid disability parking permit so don't forget it! Check with the guys at the Auto Plaza for directions.

Wheelchairs can be hired from the same place as baby buggies, near the park entrances (you've got to a have major credit card or Disney Resort ID). They are really worth getting to get around the parks and for comfortable queueing. One important thing to know is that the lovely cast members are NOT allowed to transfer people from wheelchairs to rides, so someone else in the group must be able to do this.

Enjoying Yourself

This is what it is all about and nothing should stop you from having the best time ever! Loads of the attractions have slight adaptions to make them open to all so there is no excuse - ask Guest Services to help you locate the places suitable for you. Then get stuck in and have the funniest, most exciting, thrilling holiday in the whole universe.

Disney® History

Imagine a world without Mickey Mouse, or Nemo, or Simba, or Snow White... being a kid just wouldn't be the same. But how did it all begin?

Twinkling Twenties

The 1920's marked the start of the fantastic Disney® Empire. Walt packed his bags and moved down to L.A. to start his film career. He created 'Mickey

DISNEY'S DREAMER...

So who is the genius behind the magical Disney empire? It is good old Walter Elias Disney, who sadly popped his clogs in 1966 without even seeing his Magic Kingdom dream come to life.

WALT'S WHAT?

Top Trivia about the top man...

- He was born in Chicago on Dec. 5, 1901.
- He wasn't much into school, only attending one year of high school.
- When he was nearly 5 he moved to Marceline in Missouri, he liked it there so much he modelled Main St USA in the parks on it.
- His favourite dinner was chilli and beans, washed down with tomato juice and soda crackers.
- Walt grew his gorgeous moustache when he was 25.
- Walt won more Oscars than anyone else, 32 in total.
- Not only did he create the first sound cartoon, he also made the first all-colour cartoon and the first animated feature length motion picture. Amazing!

Mouse' to star in his cartoon 'Steamboat Willie', the first film ever to have sound in time to the pictures. It was very successful for Walt and his brother Roy and signalled the start of the greatness that was to come.

Flirty Thirties
It was Oscar-tastic for Walt in the 30's. Every year for a decade Disney won the Academy Award for Best Cartoon.

Life was hard in America in the 1930's, but not for Walt and Roy. In 1937, Snow White hit the cinemas and soon became the highest grossing film of all time - pretty cool stuff.

Fighting Forties
Just when Disney® films were hitting the big time, World War 2 took place limiting the viewers, especially abroad. Disney ended up making news and educational films and found it hard to get back to the pre-war successes.

Why was Cinderella so bad at sport? Because her coach was a pumpkin!

Fantastic Fifties
1950 was a turning point for the company - hurrah! The first completely live action film, 'Treasure Island' was a huge success as was the first Disney Christmas special and the cartoon 'Cinderella'.

Walt began to tell others about his dream to create an enchanting place where both adults and children could live the Disney® magic. In 1955, his dream became reality. The first Disneyland Park® and the world's first ever theme park opened in California, a brilliant success. Walt was inspired, wanting to build them all over the world.

WAS WALT FROZEN?

Rumour has it that when Walt Disney died he was frozen, just in case they find a cure for what he died of... This urban legend has been dismissed by many 'cos apparently the first attempts at freezing a person weren't even discussed until after Walt's death, but you never know. Never say never...

Super Sixties
The sixties saw the launch of the amazing

'Mary Poppins' film, the cute Love Bug series and the planning for the Florida parks. Disney were able to buy a massive plot of land, much bigger than California and Walt started designing the park of his dreams. Sadly, he never saw it finished, he died on Dec 15th 1966.

Celebratory Seventies
1971 saw the opening of the wondrous Orlando theme park - the best park in the world. Sadly 1971 also was when Walt's brother Roy died, just after the park opened. Thankfully development continued. One of Walt Disney's last plans had been for the Experimental Prototype Community of Tomorrow, or EPCOT, as he called it. Everyone agreed this was a fab idea and in 1979 ground building started on the new park.

Experimental Eighties
The EPCOT park finally opened in 1982, a state of the art, futuristic, innovation extravaganza, there was nothing like it and there still isn't.

Just 7 years later Disney's MGM Studios opened it's doors, 135 acres dedicated to Hollywood classic movies and popular TV entertainment.

Nahtazu Nineties
It didn't finish there! The nineties saw the arrival of 'Blizzard Beach' water park, Downtown Disney and the World of Sports Complex. The best came in 1998, when Florida met Africa savannah and Disney's Animal

TRIVIAL TREE-VIA

The Animal Kingdom Tree of Life is 44m tall, and the trunk is over 15m wide. There are more than 320 animals carved into the trunk and over 103,000 leaves on approx 8,000 branches.

Kingdom opened. Just remember it is 'Nahtazu' (or not a zoo), but an amazing wildlife experience with more than 1,700 animals representing 250 different species. One of the best places to visit - big wow-appeal.

Naughty Noughties
And it didn't even stop there... whilst there hasn't been any new parks recently there have been major refurbs of some of the rides and a few fantastic arrivals. Mission:SPACE in Epcot opened in 2003 and is just amazing... Stitch's Great Escape! opened in the Magic Kingdom in 2004. 2005 sees a brilliant new water ride 'Crush 'n' Gusher' at Typhoon Lagoon water park and 'Soarin'' at Epcot . One of the most exciting new developments is 'Expedition Everest' open in the Animal Kingdom in 2006 - a thrill-a-minute coaster on a daring adventure through rugged terrain, along icy mountain ledges and inside dark snowy caves in the forbidden mountain. Wowwww!

Disney World Resort® Facts
It might have 'it's a small world in it' - but it's a pretty huge world really. The Walt Disney World Resort is over 47 square miles in size, about the same size as the whole of Greater Manchester, enormous! This is filled with 4 theme parks, 2 water-parks, 30 resort hotels, 6 golf courses, 2 shopping /dining/ fun centres and... just so much keeping over 60,000 "cast members" (that's Disney-speak for workers) busy catering to millions of guests every year. But less than 1/4 of the space has been used up so there is plenty of room for even more excitement!

Try this tongue twister 'Can you imagine an imaginary menagerie manager imagining managing an imaginary menagerie?'

WDW
FACT FILE

T
H
E

F
A
C
T
S

- All staff, oops sorry, cast members must attend the Disney University where they are taught never to cross their arms or point, not to be seen slouching or sitting down and that tattoos, red nail polish & facial hair are decorations of the devil.

- It was originally to be called 'Disney World', but when Walt popped his clogs in 1966, his bro' Roy renamed it 'Walt Disney World' ®so that everyone remembered whose dream it was to make it real.

- The Animal Kingdom is the biggest park at a whopping 500 acres.

- Summit Plummet at Blizzard Beach is the highest and fastest flume ride in the USA, where you can reach speeds of 55mph - phewww!

- Mickey Mouse has more than 175 different costumes beaten by Minnie who has more than 200 outfits (typical girl!).

- Visitors slurp more than 46 million cokes, gobble 7 million hamburgers, 5 million hot dogs and 5 million pounds of French Fries every year. Hungry?

- Christmas Day is the busiest day of the year at WDW.

- Lawnmowers at WDW mow 450,000 miles a year, the same as 18 trips around the earth.

- There is a whole other world under Magic Kingdom where the cast members hang out. The secret passageways let them get from one area to another without you seeing them!

- The World of Disney Store at the Marketplace, is the largest Disney shop in the world. It is full of Hidden Mickey's...

- WDW has Florida's two highest "mountains!" Big Thunder Mountain rises 60m & Space Mountain is 55m tall.

HIDDEN
MICKEY'S...

Some say there are hidden mickey's all over the WDW® Parks. They started out as a joke amongst Disney Imagineers. who'd add a Mickey Mouse head and ears silhouette to places, just to see if anyone noticed. Now finding hidden mickey's is a secret past-time for avid Disney fans! See if you spot any in WDW, tell us if you do!

33

HANGING OUT - WDW...

H A N G I N G O U T

Walt Disney World® Resort

4 amazing theme parks, 2 funky water parks, a huge sports complex and a pleasure park with the biggest arcade ever, loads of groovy hotels and hang outs, places to shop 'til you drop... where do you start?

PARK LIFE

● Magic Kingdom®

As you walk through the park gates it feels like you have been sprinkled with fairy dust. The beautiful castle twinkles in the distance as you trot up Main St USA you just can't stop yourself from grinning from ear to ear. 7 different lands await you each with their own charms and thrills. Head straight to Frontierland and go anti-clockwise from there to Adventureland and Tomorrowland ending in Fantasyland (heaven for littlies).

● MGM Studios

This is where film meets thrills, you feel like you are on the most exciting movie set ever. Don't miss the terrifying Twilight Zone Tower of Terror and Rock 'n' Roller Coaster and definitely go on the Tram Tour for all the insider secrets. Leave the shows (Like 'Who Wants To Be A Millionaire') for after lunch.

● EPCOT®

This is the land of discovery, where you can find out about the natural world (fab aquarium), the cultural world (cute little country sets - check out the British pub!) and tomorrow's world in an amazing lakeside setting. Quite grown up and cool in the evening.

● Animal Kingdom®

Where else can you put your nose to within a few centimetres of a hippo's guargantuan gob or a tiger's clenching claw (with a bit glass in between!)? A truly amazing place with riveting River Rapids and an unforgetable safari all under the carefully carved branches of the stunning tree of life.

● Blizzard Beach / Typhoon Lagoon

Go surfin' USA style at the wonderful Disney waterparks. Some of the slides are so scary you'll squirm but the settings are stunning, the best places to chill and get that tan going.

● Downtown Disney / Wide World Of Sport Complex

Get down at Downtown Disney, the nightly hotspot for kids of all ages and don't miss out the mega Disneyquest arcade. Check out the Wide World of Sports - you might catch some baseball!

34

©Disney

MAGIC KINGDOM PARK

EPCOT

DOWNTOWN DISNEY AREA

DISNEY'S TYPHOON LAGOON WATER PARK

OSCEOLA PARKWAY

DISNEY-MGM STUDIOS

DISNEY'S WIDE WORLD OF SPORTS COMPLEX

U.S. 192

DISNEY'S BLIZZARD BEACH WATER PARK

DISNEY'S ANIMAL KINGDOM THEME PARK

FUN-KEY!

As well as telling you about the rides and shows, we have also used icons, so you can see at a glance what the thing is like – see the key at the bottom of the page. They are:

🎧	Height restriction	🌀	Thrilling
☠	Spooky		Theatrical
🔊	Noisy	🕊	Gentle
♿	Wheelchair access	💧	Wet!
🕐	Set times		

Also look for the overall rating where we give a thumbs ups mark :

👍👍👍👍👍	Unforgettable, unbelievable, unmissable
👍👍👍👍	Wicked, one to have on the 'must do' list
👍👍👍	Pretty good
👍👍	OK, but won't set the world alight
👍	Pretty rubbish
👎	Totally rubbish, only go to laugh at it!

Remember this is just our opinion, you might not agree. If you don't then drop us a line at 💻www.knapsackguides.com. Also, most of the 👍👍👍👍👍 rides will be really popular so make sure you go there first or use a Fastpass if you can.

We've tried to make WDW as simple to understand as poss (not easy!!) - we have a section on each park and then cover the top rides (bet you can't wait for these), top sights, shows , parades and top nosh. That should have it covered - if you think we've missed anything then let us know!

Hanging Out - Magic Kingdom®
Top Rides
Splash Mountain®

🔲 Frontierland®
🎧 1.02m
🕐 🌀 💧 Fastpass
Rating: 👍👍👍👍

A true Disney® classic. Combining a couple of tummy tickling, splashing drops with the cute the-atre and story of Brer

Rabbit (that's a bit babyish...) you'll be whooping one minute and aaahhing the next. The biggest thrill is the 5 storey, 40 mile per hour waterfall drop, exciting, especially as it comes as a bit of a surprise after all of the story telling!

Big Thunder Mountain

Frontierland®
1.02m
ℹ️ 📷 🔊 Fastpass
Rating: ♦♦♦

Hang on to your hats as the runaway miner's train zips through the amazing setting of a deserted mining town in the wicked Wild West. This rickety roller coaster is a great ride, jerky but jolly and long enough that you feel the queuing was worth it. Definitely one not to miss.

Space Mountain®

Tomorrowland®
1.12m
ℹ️ 📷 🔊 Fastpass
Rating: ♦♦♦

The scariest ride in the Magic Kingdom, but good scary (there are wilder thrills in other parks). You zip around the bends at 28 miles per hour, plunging down and shooting up in the pitch black darkness. Watch out for passing rockets - get the front seat for the most exciting ride.

QUEUE TIP
This is a great ride to rush to straight after the parades in the evening.

Pirates of The Caribbean

Adventureland®
ℹ️ 📷 👤 🔊 Fastpass [Hand Held Captioning Available]
Rating: ♦♦♦♦

Whilst this is gentle it is quite magical and more than a little spooky, worth going on a couple of times to

Height restriction   Thrilling   Spooky   Theatrical
Noisy   Wet   Gentle   Wheelchair access   Set times

make sure you catch it all. Cruel, rowdy pirates living in the secret dingy depths of the Caribbean under-world cheer, jeer and joke as you sail past on your boat, passing rotting skeletons, shiny treasure and scenes of skulduggery and treachery. There are a couple of fun splashes too as you drop into the caverns. Disney audio-animatronics at it's very best. Excellent!

Buzz Lightyear's Space Ranger Spinner

Tomorrowland®
Fastpass [Hand Held Captioning Available]
Rating: ◊◊◊◊

Cartoon meets ride meets arcade game in this fun alien chasing spintacular. Under the command of Buzz Lightyear you become a Junior Space Ranger on a mission to laser cannon   targets that zap the enemy Zurg's power. You're told your score at the end, you do get better with a bit of prac-tise - see if you can beat the grown ups!

BUZZ ON...
"On the Buzz ride, aim for the little 'Z's,' they have the most points. Hit them over and over and over"

Haunted Mansion

Liberty Square
Rating: ◊◊◊

As you enter the manic mansion you are ushered into a round room and wel-comed; then as the room mysteriously starts to stretch you plunge deep into the house (with a few surprises on the way!). Then stroll along the haunt-ed corridor and climb into one of the 130 "doom bug-gies" to begin the toe curling tour. Good fun with ace audio-animatronic effects and not really that scary unless you are wheasly wimp - don't shut your eyes, there is too much to see. Very similar to 'Phantom Manor' at Disneyland Resort Paris.

Why are ghosts bad at telling lies ? Because you can see right through them !

Top Sights, Shows & Parades

Mickey's PhilarMagic

Fantasyland®

ⓘ 🎭 ✂ 🕐 ♿ Fastpass
Rating: ◔◔◔◔

Watch daft Donald get into the doo doo when his directing of the orchestra goes oh soooo wrong in this newish 3D mega movie extravaganza. Loads of the Disney faves pop out at you from the massive screen; Mickey, Aladdin, Ariel & Simba all make an appearance in this tame but funny family favourite. A good one for ALL the family (even your scaredy cat grandma).

Stitch's Great Escape ™

Tomorrowland®
♁ 95cm
ⓘ 🎭 ◁᎑ Fastpass
Rating: ◔◔◔

Be prepared for a few (smelly) surprises when you take charge of the

YUCCKKY!

Stitch is the first Audio-Animatronics® character that spits! Nice...

mischievous 'Experiment 626' (aka Stitch) in the pre-quel to the famous 'Lilo & Stitch' film.

Kind of in between a ride and a show, this hilarious adventure is funny and thrilling. Stitch will make you look like an angel, remember to point this out to the grown ups!

Cinderella's Surprise Celebration

Right outside the Castle
Rating: ◔◔◔

A good time to meet the characters as well as ooohhh and aaaahh as Cinders and her buddies sing their hearts out in a magical, musical, mystical, melodious melodrama - quite marvellous! If this is your kind of thing you'll also love Cinderellabration, where you can see Cinders being crowned with the priceless princess tiara.

What did Cinderella sing when her photographs weren't ready?
One day my prints will come!

♁ Height restriction   🎭 Thrilling   🕷 Spooky   🎭 Theatrical
◁᎑ Noisy   💧 Wet   Gentle   ♿ Wheelchair access   🕐 Set times

Share A Dream Come True Parade

Main Street USA® and Frontierland®
Rating: 🌀🌀🌀🌀🌀

This is the classic Disney parade with Mickey, Minnie and all of the favourites on the huge floats featuring huge snow domes with dancing, prancing princesses and cute cuddly characters striding the streets. Phototastic!

SpectroMagic Parade

Main Street USA®
Rating: 🌀🌀🌀🌀🌀

It's just so pretty, so sparkly you'll love it. Taking place only on special ocassions it is well worth attending. The 20-minute spectacular has twinkly fibre optics, groovy holographic images, clouds of liquid nitrogen, and loads of little lights made all the more magical by the jolly Disney tunes. Chernabog, Fantasia's monstrous demon unfolds his whopping 11.5m wingspan - cooooel.

PAL MICKEY

This amazing talking Mickey Mouse toy acts as a hilarious tour guide bringing each of the four main WDW theme parks, Magic Kingdom, Epcot, Disney-MGM Studios and Disney's Animal Kingdom to life. Using wireless technology he knows where you are and what time it is - v. clever stuff! Costs c. $60.

DID YOU KNOW?

It takes the same electricity as seven lightning bolts to bring Spectromagic to life.

Wishes™ Nighttime Spectacular

Cinderella's Castle - best view = bottom Main Street USA
Rating: 🌀🌀🌀🌀

Probably the best firework display you will ever see or have ever seen in your life - honest! Jiminy Cricket tells the story of how dreams come true with favourites Pinocchio, Cinderella, Ariel and Peter

Pan taking centre stage under the breathtaking sparkling explosions. You'll be wowed, prepare to be impressed.

Top Nosh

Cinderella's Royal Table
Inside the Wondrous Castle
Rating: ◇◇◇◇

Smile nicely as Cinders welcomes you into her dining room. Especially cool for a character breakfast, this is a popular choice so best use the priority seating service. Puds are ace - try the choc brownie mousse.

Tony's Town Square Restaurant
Town Square, Main Street USA®
Rating: ◇◇◇

If you are a pasta fan then get yourself down to Tony's for spaghetti and meatballs, the fave of the Lady and the Tramp who rule the roost here. The mouse-shaped pizzas are a good filler.

Liberty Tree Tavern
Liberty Square
Rating: ◇◇◇◇

All American fare here, salads and sandwiches for lunch and a nice turkey dinner in the evening! Minnie and her mates invite you to their historic character meals, as usual you'd best book in advance.

SNACK ATTACK
Where do you get the best of your faves?

Fruit / Healthy Stuff	Toontown Farmer's Market
Buffet	Crystal Palace (see what you eat!!)
Burgers	Pecos Bill Cafe
Chips	Frontierland Fries
Drinks	Cool Ship
Sweets	Main Street Confectionery
Ice Cream	Aloha Isle / Mrs. Potts' Cupboard
Super Slushes	Enchanted Grove
Puds / Cakes	Main Street Bakery

A bizarre Disney delicacy is a huge smoked Turkey leg, look disgusting but seem very popular. Do you dare down one?

⦿ Height restriction   ☑ Thrilling   ♨ Spooky   ☍ Theatrical
◂�))) Noisy   ● Wet   ◐ Gentle   ♿ Wheelchair access   ⊕ Set times

Hanging Out - MGM Studios

This place rocks - it's quite hard core. Whether you fancy yourself as an aged hairy pop dude or a glamorous movie mogul, you'll be at home here, groov-y!

Top Rides
Twilight Zone Tower of Terror™

Sunset Boulevard
↟ 1.02m
ⓘ 🅿 ♿ ♨ Fastpass
Rating: ♦♦♦♦♦

DID YOU KNOW?

The Tower of Terror is the highest ride in the whole of WDW. It is over 60m tall – you get a fab view if you dare keep your eyes open!

One of the best rides in the parks, in America, in fact in the whole world! Every ride is unique; you go up, you go down, you even go across but you never do the same thing twice.

The queue can be long but it is ever so entertaining, especially when you get into the cobweb-ridden, scary-mary Hollywood Tower Hotel. Them staff are weird, damn weird, I hope your hotel crew have a bit more charm. After hanging out in the boiler room you clamber into the lift (luckily you get a seat!) for the jaw dropping, spine tingling, pant wetting tour of the hotel. Don't go here just after eating loads of greasy grub - it could be very messy...

Rock 'n' Roller Coaster® starring Aerosmith

Sunset Boulevard
↟ 1.22m
ⓘ 🅿 ♿ ♪ Fastpass
Rating: ♦♦♦♦♦

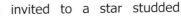

Another belter and right next door to the terror tower. Do one right after the other for a full-on thrill feast - if you dare.

There is a story to entertain you as you wait. You have been invited to a star studded

Aerosmith after show party but need to get there super quick and your running late. The pop diva limo is waiting to take you there, climb in and prepare to be thrilled.

This is no ordinary coaster, from the super-g start to the flips and spins of the speediest track, all to the ear bursting guitar rifts from the Aerosmith gang; it's soooperb.

LAST RESORT

We are nothing if not honest... so we thought we'd tell you the things best avoided...

- The Great Movie Ride - only great 'cos it's in a big room, dull, boring and disappointing.
- Walt Disney: One Man's Dream - OK , so he was an amazing, magical man who invented this wondrous place, but you're not really here for a history lesson.
- Voyage Of The Little Mermaid - this is highly acclaimed & has ace special effects, but it is made for really little kids...

Disney-MGM Backlot Tour
Mickey Avenue
ⓘ 📷 ♿ ♦
Rating: ♦♦♦♦

Fancy a sneak behind the scenes? Always wanted to know how they make the movies so magnificant and so real? Well this is the place to find out. Part ride, part show, you can even have a leading film role. Actually why not volunteer the oldies, there is a good chance they'll get soaking wet (don't tell them that, might put them off!).

This place is actually real - they do make movies and TV shows here as well as create amazing costumes and spectacular props and special effects. Watch out when you get to Catastrophe Canyon, it's a little surprising...

Where do Martians drink beer? At a Mars bar !

Star Tours
Streets of America
♀ 1.02m
ⓘ 📷 ♿ Fastpass
Rating: ♦♦♦

If you are a space fiend then get on down to Star Tours for a 7 minute intergalatic mystery

43

♀ Height restriction 📷 Thrilling ☆ Spooky ☁ Theatrical
🔊 Noisy ♦ Wet ✋ Gentle ♿ Wheelchair access ⏰ Set times

tour with the accident prone, clumsy Captain Rex. Hang onto your seat belt as you zoom towards the death star - the special effects are amazing, it feels <u>so</u> real even though never leave the ground. A must for Star Wars fans, you can even have a photo taken with R2D2 or C3PO.

Top Sights, Shows & Parades

Indiana Jones™ Epic Stunt Spectacular

Streets of America
ⓘ 📷 👷 🕐 ♿ Fastpass
Rating: ♦♦♦

DID YOU KNOW?
The giant rolling ball that threatens to crush Indy is 4m wide and weighs nearly 200kg. About the same as a male lion!

Another chance for the oldies to take to the stage in a thrilling stunt extravaganza (pity kids aren't allowed, it'd be much better, but apparently it's "too dangerous..."). With fire, explosions, massive rolling rocks and viscious vagabonds to contend with it's all go for the dashing hero Indiana Jones.

Not only do you see the show, you also find out a few tricks of the trade, watching action heroes will never be the same. Don't try them out at home though - it might look easy but you don't want to end up splatted do you?

Who Wants To Be A Millionaire-Play It!

Mickey Avenue
ⓘ 📷 👷 🕐 ♿ Fastpass
Rating: ♦♦♦

Have a go at winning the million, well beating your family anyway. It's just like the studio you see on TV, same couple of chairs in the middle, but EVERYONE plays the 'fastest finger first' bit. Whoever answers first gets to join the host in the

GO FOR IT!
Everyone has the same chance to get on the hot seat - even if you don't know the answers just press 4 random letters (DCAB) as quickly as you can, you might get it right!

hot seat and can win prizes like Disney baseball caps and badges, not exactly millions but fun anyway.

Beauty & The Beast - Live On Stage
⌐ Sunset Boulevard
ⓘ ⚲ ♿
Rating: ◊◊◊

Did you enjoy the film? If so, then you'll love this. Settle down with Belle and friends after a few of the scary rides, for a half hour musical, theatrical treat that'll have you smiling and clapping in no time!

HIDDEN MICKEYS

- The actual stage area for the B&B show is a huge hidden mickey.
- Check out the wet patch on the workman's shirt, you may see another...

Jim Henson's Muppet Vision 3D
⌐ Streets of America
ⓘ ⚲ ♿
Rating: ◊◊◊◊

Where does Kermit keep his dosh? In a river bank.

Don't rush to get to the front in this 3 (or 4) dimensional spectacular, some of the best views are from the middle of the back! Fozzie Bear kicks off with a 10 minute hilarious pre-show before the 20 minute main event in a theatre, just like the one in the Muppet Show itself. Miss Piggy and Kermit take you on a tour of the Muppet Labs with hilarious consequences and stunning effects. Keep your eyes open for off-stage action - that mad chef is up to mischief in the back...

Lights, Motors, Action!™ Extreme Stunt Show
⌐ Streets of America
ⓘ ⚠ ♿ ⏲
Rating: ◊◊◊◊

Brought over from Disneyland Resort Paris© 'cos it is so ace, this motor stunt fiesta cer-

---

❂ Height restriction   ⚠ Thrilling   ☲ Spooky   ⚲ Theatrical
⁕ Noisy   ● Wet   ⋎ Gentle   ♿ Wheelchair access   ⏲ Set times

tainly is an all action attraction. Squealing wheels, screeching brakes and roaring engines fill the arena making you gasp in amazement and dream of being a stuntman or woman.

MEETING CHARACTERS

Having your pic. taken with one of the Disney characters is a must-do activity no matter how old you are, honest! These are good character meeting hints, remember you may need to queue:

- The hotel foyers at the WDW Resort hotels.
- At the Character Breakfasts in hotels and park restaurants.
- Check out Time Guides on Maps for meeting sess's in the parks.
- Arrive early at the parks, characters often entertain early arrivers and it's quite quiet!

Fantasmic!
Hollywood Hills Amphitheartre
Rating: ✦✦✦✦
MGM's evening firework, laser and musical pageant is pretty fantasmic as the name suggests. Telling the stories of Mickey's manic dreams and featuring many of the Disney villians, it is quite amazing and sometimes a little scary (if you are a wimp...). Some say it is the best show at WDW so it is really popular, get there early to be sure of top seats in the waterfront Hollywood amphitheatre.

Why would you put sugar under your pillow?
To have sweet dreams!

Top Nosh
Sci-Fi Dine-In Theatre
Commissary Lane
Rating: ✦✦✦✦
One of the coolest cafes ever invented. Slide into a snazzy car lined up at the drive-in movie (get the back seat, you can annoy the person in front) and tuck into the kid's menu. OK, the food's not that exciting but it is

What's the best day to eat bacon?
Fry-day.

served in a 'glow in the dark' frisbee whilst waitresses rollerskate by and black and white films flicker in the background.

Fifties Prime Time Cafe
⊡ Echo Lake
Rating: ♦♦♦

Funky, kitsch and kind of cool, grab some macaroni and a milkshake in a kitchen like your granny had. Watch out for the waitresses, they act like they're your mum and

FOOD FUN!
You can buy fake flies or bugs at a joke shop. Put a couple in the salad.
Gummy worms have a similar effect, go for the brown / black ones, they look more real.

try to feed you your dinner like a train, you know 'choo choo open the tunnel' and all that! Lots of fun and very busy so book priority seating.

The Hollywood Brown Derby
⊡ By The Sorceror's Hat
Rating: ♦♦♦

This is the swanky option, a proper sit-down star spangled restaurant with famous faces peering at you from around the walls. One of the finest places to eat in terms of posh nosh, and not just for grown ups. The kids menu is pretty damn scrumptious, especially the puds. Somewhere to go for a special treat.

SNACK ATTACK
Where do you get the best of your faves?

Fruit / Healthy Stuff	Anaheim Produce
Buffet / PYO	Sunset Ranch Market
Burgers	ABC Commissary / Backlot Express
Chips	Fairfax Fries
Drinks	Peevys Polar Pipeline (coo-el)
Milkshake	Min & Bill's Dockside Diner
Ice Cream	Dinosaur Gertie's
Puds / Cakes	Starring Rolls Cafe

♀ Height restriction 🎢 Thrilling 👻 Spooky 🎭 Theatrical
📢 Noisy 💧 Wet 🎡 Gentle ♿ Wheelchair access 🕐 Set times

Hanging Out - EPCOT®

A park of 2 halves this one - the science / land of tomorrow bit 'Future World' and then the 'World Showcase', the mini country settings around the lake. A little bizzare perhaps, but well worth a visit nevertheless 'cos it has two of the best rides ever...

Top Rides

Mission: SPACE
Future World
↻ 1.12m
ⓘ 📷 ↻ ☂ Fastpass
Rating: ☺☺☺☺☺

BE IN COMMAND...
When you enter the holding area stand in the second space from the front - then you will get to be commander!

This is a MUST DO. If your wildest dream is to be an astronaut or if you love adrenaline rides then this is the place to go. The build up in the queuing area is really informative all about space travel history, preparing you for the background to your mission. Anticipation builds further as you enter the briefing area, you feel like you are really, really going to space. The ride itself is totally thrilling - feel the 'g' man! We won't give too much away except to say that this is truly fantastic. It just feels so real, the pull of the gravity, the speed, the weightlessness, go there first. Not good for vommers.

The advance training area at the end is also worth spending some time at, some funky photo ops.

Spaceship Earth
Future World
ⓘ 📷 ↻
Rating: ☺☺☺

MICKEY SPOTTING!
Look up in the starry sky just after you get on the ride for a Mickey constellation.

This ride is getting on a bit nowadays, but it is still a laugh. Your 'time machine' takes you on a 15 minute trip up the 18 storeys of the massive EPCOT golf ball and through thousands of years of history. Some say it is a little boring, not worth a huge wait, but give it a go in the afternoon when it gets quieter.

Test Track

⌐ Future World
⌐ 1.02m
ⓘ 🚗 ◄» Fastpass
Rating: ◊◊◊◊◊

Another unmissable attraction, excellent from start to finish. Find out about the history of car development and safety testing - more interesting than it sounds. You queue indoors in the testing area so there is lots to look at and learn about. Climb into your car, buckle up and get ready to be the ultimate crash test dummy.

Hang on tight, this baby knows how to move and you are NOT in control. It goes so fast - the 5 1/2 minutes disappear in a haze as you zip around at up to 60mph. Groovy! Loads more stuff after the ride - see the car of the future and sit in a few cool cars of today.

Soarin'™

⌐ Future World
ⓘ 🌾 Fastpass
Rating: ◊◊◊

Fancy flying over California? Built in 2005 to celebrate the "Happiest Celebration on Earth," (50 years of Disney theme parks) this is a copy of the Disneyland California ride. Get a bird's eye view of good old Cali as you and 87 others are carried more than 12 metres high over the mountains, the desert and the sea. But it's not just what you see that makes this cool, it's also what you feel, smell and hear so keep all your senses on full alert!

> What do you get if your budgie flies into the blender? Shredded Tweet!

⌐ Height restriction   🚗 Thrilling   ☃ Spooky   ⌐ Theatrical
◄» Noisy   ◆ Wet   🌾 Gentle   ♿ Wheelchair access   ⓘ Set times

Living With The Land

Future World
ⓘ Fastpass
Rating: ◊◊◊

A disaster at the start - you might wonder why you bothered. But then it gets soooooo much better when you sail through the food science experimental zone where Disney has joined with leading edge partners to develop exciting farming and food technology. They have even managed to get marrows to grow just from fresh air, amazing. Especially if you live in the third world where the soil is really poor, or even if you live in outer space and have no soil at all! You'll learn lots on this 'ride', keep your eyes and ears open. If the queue is more than 20 mins use Fastpass & go to 'The Sea' first - this can save lots of time.

DID YOU KNOW?

Last year, more than 30 tons (27,000 kg) of fruits and veggies were harvested from The Land's gardens.

Top Sights, Shows & Parades

The Living Seas

Future World
ⓘ
Rating: ◊◊◊◊

A very boring start, queuing in a dark tunnel with not very interesting pictures on the walls - but hang in there, it is worth the wait. Don't miss the intro. presentation it sets the scene nicely. Then descend to the depths of the ocean, via the hydrospheres, where you can see amazing sea life including the cutest dolphins ever. Don't miss Bruce's Shark World or 'Turtle Talk with Crush', both great. This place is like a funky Sea Life centre but better - the aquarium is one of the biggest in the world (Spaceship Earth could fit inside it!!). A great place to cool down when the rays are beating down.

Try this tongue twister... "Six sharp smart sharks"

Innoventions

Future World

Rating:

Some bits of this are fab, some things a little dull so pick and choose where you spend time. Split into 2 areas (East & West), each filled with hands-on gadgets and gizmos. The best bits include a chance to test the latest computer and video games - watch as the grown ups look dumbfounded! You can also send emails home for free so take your mate's email addresses with you and set up a mobile email address, that will really impress them.

World Showcase

World Showcase Lagoon

[NOTE - Doesn't open until 11am]

Rating:

You might get a bit bored here - it is not a thrill a minute. But it is interesting, a good place to wander around in the evening and perhaps get something 'exotic' to eat before or after watching the fireworks. It's an opportunity to visit 11 countries without leaving the US of A. Most pavilions are hosted by locals so if you'd like to learn a little Japanese or Italian this could be your chance!

PASS - PORTS

The places featured in the World Showcase are:

- Mexico
- China
- Italy
- Japan
- France
- Norway
- Germany
- USA
- Morocco
- UK
- Canada

Height restriction · Thrilling · Spooky · Theatrical
Noisy · Wet · Gentle · Wheelchair access · Set times

Illuminations: Reflections of Earth

⬛ World Showcase Lagoon
Rating: ◊◊◊◊

The firework and special effect show at EPCOT is just brilliant, taking place right in the middle of the huge lake. Telling the story of the creation of the earth, it is pretty spectular, it lasts 15 minutes and uses up 2,800 fireworks. Get there early to get a good viewing spot.

Top Nosh

The Garden Grill Restaurant

⬛ Land Pavilion
ⓘ See Chip & Dale and Farmer Mickey
Rating: ◊◊◊

Sample some of the fruits of the Land in this healthier than usual restaurant. Serving good old American favourites like chicken and chips and macaroni cheese you can't go wrong. You can also watch the 'Living with the Land' ride float by, get a good seat.

The Coral Reef Restaurant

⬛ Living Seas
Rating: ◊◊◊◊

Get a seat downstairs by the tanks so that you can watch the sealife swim by as you get stuck in - can put you off the fish fingers a bit though! Seafood is the speciality here, very scrummy and a little grown up. Ask for a fish identification card so you can tell what's what.

Nine Dragons

⬛ China, World Showcase Lagoon
Rating: ◊◊◊

Tasty oriental treats and very friendly staff make this a good choice, especially for a yummy lunch. They also have a kids menu and a kid's cocktail 'China Doll' - a must have! Sometimes the chefs put on a show, worth looking out for.

Why did the dragon go on a diet? It weighed too much for its scales!

52

Teppanyaki Dining Room
⬚ Japan, World Showcase Lagoon
Rating: ◊◊◊

The closest you'll get to having your own personal chef! This is similar to a restaurant that Posh and Beck's take their kids too so it can't be bad. You pick what you'd like (veggie, chicken, steak etc) and the chef whips it up on a hot plate right in front of you.

San Angel Inn
⬚ Mexico, World Showcase Lagoon
Rating: ◊◊◊◊

Sit alongside the Mexican river (actually the El Rio del Tiempo ride) and tuck into nachos and chilli. Make sure you request a table on the water when you arrive.

MEXMAX

Try these yummy Mexican treats:

- Quesadilla - grilled cheese (+chicken) tortilla sandwich
- Burritto - deep fried filled tortilla
- Nachos - tortilla chips with cheese & chilli topping

Biergarten
⬚ Germany, World Showcase Lagoon
Rating: ◊◊◊◊

Go here in the evening and tuck into the buffet (see before you eat) celebrating the marriage of Crown Prince Ludwig of Bavaria whilst enjoying the yodelers and the noisy oompah band! A good fun night out.

FOOD GURU

Where do you get the rest of your faves?

Healthy Stuff	Sunshine Season Food Fair, Land
Character Brekkie	Akershus, Norway
Burgers	Liberty Inn, USA
Fish 'n' Chips	Harry Ramsden's, UK
Drinks	Ice Station Cool
General Goodies	Refreshment Port
Puds / Cakes	Boulangerie Patisserie, France

🎧 Height restriction   🎢 Thrilling   ☻ Spooky   Theatrical
🔊 Noisy   ♦ Wet   Gentle   ♿ Wheelchair access   🕐 Set times

Hanging Out - Animal Kingdom

The best 'not a zoo' in the whole world. This is a magic kingdom, a must for all animal lovers.

Top Rides
Kilimanjaro Safaris®
Africa
ⓘ ☑ Fastpass
Rating: ◊◊◊◊◊

You are so going to enjoy this. Jump on board the safari wagon for a fantastic jungle adventure where you will see hippos, lions, elephants, rhino to name a few. Just when you are thinking how fab it is, things take a slight change in direction in more ways than one. Hold on tight!

Kali River Rapids®
Asia
⌂ 0.97m
ⓘ ☑ Fastpass
Rating: ◊◊◊

Time to cool off in the white water raft escapade! It might start off as a gentle paddle down the Chakranadi river, but before you know it you'll be spinning and bumping along the rapids and cruising through the pouring waterfalls. You'll get drenched - so be prepared and enjoy it.

Expedition Everest™
Asia
⌂ 0.97m
ⓘ ☑ ⌄ ⚠ Fastpass
Rating: ◊◊◊◊◊

How did the yeti feel when he had flu? Abominable!!

This amazing new high-speed train adventure opens in 2006. Combining coaster-like thrills with the excitement of a close encounter with the Yeti, it takes you to another dimension. Climbing up the highest mountain created by the Disney imagineers is exciting enough, but the forward, backward chase to escape the abominable snowman tops it all. Thrill-tastic!!

DINOSAUR

⌁ DinoLand USA
⌀ 1.02m
ⓘ 🎢 ◀)) ⚇ Fastpass
Rating: ◊◊◊◊

Zoom back 65 million years in a time machine to the dino age to save the last iguanodon. Of course this is no easy task,

TEE-HEE

Take a look at the photos on display at the end, they are hilarious! Some of the oldies look petrified!!

you'll have to brave a meteor shower, a very jerky ride and scariest of all the dripping, smoking, smelling hungry jaws of the fast, ferocious carnotaurus. Can you take it?

Top Sights, Shows & Parades

Pangani Forest Exploration Trail

⌁ Africa
ⓘ 🎢 ☿ ♿
Rating: ◊◊◊◊

So much more exciting than it sounds! This is like a walking safari, you get so close to the animals your eyes will pop out of your head. Sometimes you are just so close to big scary beasts like hippos and gorillas, with just a glass wall separating you, truly wicked. It's also really pretty, especially in the Gorilla gorge.

Maharaja Jungle Trek

⌁ Asia
ⓘ 🎢 ☿ ♿
Rating: ◊◊◊◊

Finish off the nature trails with a wander around the regal Anandapur forest meeting funny creatures like the hanging fruit bats and amazing beauties like the

⌀ Height restriction   🎢 Thrilling   ⚇ Spooky   Theatrical
◀)) Noisy   ♦ Wet   Gentle   ♿ Wheelchair access   Set times

stunning royal tigers basking in their crumbling majestic sanctuary. The largest lizards in the world are worth a snoop - Komodo dragons are well ugly!

It's Tough To Be A Bug!®

Discovery Island

ⓘ 🎦 ☼ ⊙ ♿
Rating: ◊◊◊◊

"It's Tough To Be A Bug!" based upon the Disney / Pixar film "A Bug's Life" ©Disney / Pixar

If you like 'A Bug's Life' you will love this. The queue takes you into the roots of the amazing tree of life (how many animals can you spot?) and into the dark theatre. Pop on your bug-eye 3D goggles and be transported to insect life for a fun adventure with a few surprises along the way!

Festival of the Lion King

Camp Minnie-Mickey

ⓘ 🎦 ☼ ⊙ ♿
Rating: ◊◊◊◊

What games do ants play with elephants? Squash!

As good as you get in the West End of London, this fast-moving, magical, musical mayhem completely rocks. Featuring all of the favourites from the film in terms of characters and songs, you'll be singing 'Hakuna Matata' for the rest of the day.

DID YOU KNOW?

During 'Hakuna Matata' in the Lion King film, Timon pulls a bug out of the log wearing Mickey ears.

Jammin' Jungle Parade

Around Discovery Island

ⓘ 🎦 ☼ ⊙ ♿
Rating: ◊◊◊

Watch Mickey and his mates as they pass by in an assortment of jungle buggies accompanied by puppets, stiltwalkers and of course, funky jungle beats!

Lucky the Dinosaur

⌖ Around DinoLand

ⓘ ☺ ♿
Rating: ◊◊◊

Lucky the prehistoric animatronic dino will have you in pre-hysterics as he strolls around the park! Lucky walks on two legs, is 3m tall and 4m long, a big guy! He loves people and balloons and can sign autographs as well as laugh, sneeze, bellow and occasionally gets hiccups - good that's all, imagine dino farts - yuk!

Top Nosh

There is only really one 'proper' restaurant in the Animal Kingdom, the rest are takeaways and cafes. Luckily that doesn't matter 'cos the Rainforest Cafe is the only place you'd want to go anyway!

Rainforest Cafe

⌖ Just inside the entrance to the Animal Kingdom
Rating: ◊◊◊◊

Fab food, fantastic setting, funny elephants, friendly staff - this is the best place to eat in the Animal Kingdom. It is a real treat to go to this place anytime, but the way it just so fits with the location makes it even better! You might have to queue, but it is worth it. Truly, truly scrumptious.

QUEUE TIP

The restaurant does get busy, but there are often seats at the bar. It's also fun sitting up on one of the big bar stools!

SCOOBIE SNACKS

Don't feed the animals, but where's the human nosh?

Healthy Stuff	Harambe Fruit Market
Character Brekkie	Restaurantosaurus
Burgers	Sunaulo Toran Fries
Ice Cream	Anandapur Ice Cream
Drinks	Tamu Tamu Refreshments
Pizza	Pizzafari
Puds / Cakes	Kusafiri Bakery

ⴖ Height restriction   ⚡ Thrilling   ☠ Spooky   Theatrical
♫ Noisy   ◆ Wet   Gentle   ♿ Wheelchair access   Set times

Hanging Out - Blizzard Beach

Top Rides
Summit Plummet
⌀ 1.22m
Rating: ♦♦♦♦♦

The Ski Resort theme comes into its own on Summit Plummet. Climbing the 40m to the top is scary enough, but when the plunging drop zips you down at around 60mph (faster than Space Mountain), it is positively pant-wetting! Only the bravest need bother, many stop off at slightly tamer Slusher Gusher, that's brave enough.

TOP TRICK

Bet someone $10 that you'll do 'the big one', nodding up in the direction of Summit Plummet, then divert to Slusher Gusher. You didn't say which big one did you?

Slusher Gusher
Rating: ♦♦♦♦

This slide drops you down a snow-banked mountain gully at over 25mph. A good option if you are tempted by the mountain, Summit Plummet - an excellent and scary enough alternative.

Downhill Double Dipper
Rating: ♦♦♦

Another petrifying one! You go through a waterfall, down one tube, do a spot of free-falling and then drop down another tube to the exit. Pheww!

What's an ig ?
An eskimo's home without a loo !

Snow Stormers
Rating: ♦♦♦♦

Sled down this mock slalom on your belly, twisting through the tubes whilst the water splashes back over your face. There are 3 tubes, so you can have a race with two others.

Toboggan Racers

Rating: ◊◊◊◊

Race your mates head first down the 8-lane water slide over exhilarating dips descending the "snowy" slope. This time being porky is an advantage 'cos you go down faster!

DID YOU KNOW?

From the top of the highest slides at Blizzard Beach, you can see all 4 parks - the Tree of Life at Animal Kingdom, the Castle at Magic Kingdom, Spaceship Earth at Epcot, and the Tower of Terror at Disney-MGM Studios.

Teamboat Springs

Rating: ◊◊◊

This is the world's longest white-water raft ride that fits the whole family in the six-person raft. Then you zoom down a twisting 400m series of rushing water falls - hang on tight!

Runoff Rapids

Rating: ◊◊◊

Clamber up the back of Mount Gushmore to reach the 3 tube rides. You have to carry your raft all the way up the 157 steps, and more than once 'cos the 3 routes are slightly different!

Cross Country Creek

Rating: ◊◊◊

A cool way to chill out is to bob around the creek that surrounds the entire park. Just watch out for the ice cave - you want to chill not freeze!!

BEST OF THE REST

Sun Bathing	Melt-Away Beach
Shopping	Beach Haus
Views	Chair Lift
Fast Food	Lottawotta Lodge
Ice Cream	Freddie's Frozen Refreshments
Puds / Cakes	Warming Hut
Towel Rental	Shoeless Joe's

♁ Height restriction ◳ Thrilling ☃ Spooky ☂ Theatrical
◁» Noisy ◆ Wet ▽ Gentle ♿ Wheelchair access ⏲ Set times

Hanging Out - Typhoon Lagoon

Top Rides
Crush 'n' Gusher
⌒ 1.22m
Rating: ◊◊◊◊
The latest ride to open in Typhoon Lagoon is a first...a kind of water coaster, cool-el! Powerful water jets pro-pel your raft through cavernous twists and turns, eventually spitting you out into the tranquil waters of Hideaway Bay, exhilerated but exhausted! There are 3 different ride options, each more than 100m long. Go on all three!

Humunga Kowabunga
⌒ 1.22m
Rating: ◊◊◊◊
Another heart-stopper! The trio of gully enclosed speed slides shoot you through rocky caverns at over 30mph, scary-mary but really thrilling. Get there early, this is a popular one.

Gangplank Falls
Rating: ◊◊◊
Grab all your family for this white water rafting adventure that twists and turns through waterfalls and past the rocky out-crops. Relatively gentle, a good one if you are recovering from some of the other rides.

Why couldn't the pirate play cards? 'Cos he was sitting on the deck!

Storm Slides
Rating: ◊◊◊
A triple whammy! Three body slides corkscrew down through caves and waterfalls at speeds of about 20 mph. All 3 offer a slightly different experience...

Shark Reef
Rating: ◊◊◊◊
This is the place to learn to snorkel. Instructors are around the mini 'sea' of tropical fish, stingrays, and

leopard and bonnethead sharks (don't worry they're behind perspex!!), swimming around a sunken tanker. If you've done it before then jump right in, but remember you can't use your own gear, you've got to use Disney stuff. Get the oldies

to take your pic from the underwater viewing room in the hold of the ship.

Surf Pool

Rating: 🐾🐾🐾🐾

Jump into Florida's largest inland surfing lagoon. But watch out when you hear the foghorn, that means a huge wave is about to strike - some as high as 2m. It's quite scary, if you're not a great swimmer there is a smaller nearby lagoon.

> **SURF DUDE!**
> Early on Tues & Fri you can have surfing lessons in the huge wave pool. Surfboards are provided. You've got to be at least 8yrs old. Expensive but so COO-EL! Reserve on 407-WDW-SURF.

If swimming isn't your scene at all then chill out on one of the many loungers - you are on holiday aren't you?!

Castaway Creek

Rating: 🐾🐾🐾

If chillin's more your thing, then relax in an inner tube and get carried along by the gentle currents of Castaway Creek. Slip in at one of five entrances along the

> **FOOD DUDE!**
> Our recommendations:
> ● Low Tide Lou's
> ● Typhoon Tilly's
> ● Leaning Palms OR
> ● Bring your own picnic!

creek and bob by the waterfalls, caves, and rain forests as you drift along taking in the rays...

🔾 Height restriction   🎢 Thrilling   👻 Spooky   🎭 Theatrical
🔊 Noisy   💧 Wet   Gentle   ♿ Wheelchair access   ⏱ Set times

Hanging Out - Disney's Wide World Of Sport® Complex

If you are sporty check out the 200-acre, state-of-the-art Disney sports complex - especially if there is some action taking place. Whether professional or amateur, it's your chance to see

some U.S. sport like American football, baseball or basketball, and they are all pretty cooel.

The spectator areas are so close to the action, you almost feel you are taking part yourself! You can easily get caught up in the excitement, even if you don't quite know what is going on!

Top Training

The Atlanta Braves base-ballers have their spring training here in Feb / March, getting them in top form for the summer season.

The Tampa Bay Bucaneers, the American Football team, also hold their training camp in the summer (August).

Top Nosh
Official All Star Cafe®

Rating: ✦✦✦

Big U.S. sports stars (Andre Agassi, Monica Seles, Tiger Woods) have put their fave munchies on the yummy menu of this sports cafe. You can also see memorabilia from sporting legends (you won't know many of them) - check your shoe size against basketball supremo's Shaquille O'Neals size 22! Big or what?!

Hanging Out - DisneyQuest®

Part of Downtown Disney, this has got to be one the best arcades in the whole world. With indoor rides, virtual reality games and a few funny things to do, it's a great place to go for a change or if it rains. Best of all once you've paid most of it is free so get stuck in!

Top Rides

Cyber Space Mountain
↔ 1.30m
Rating: ◊◊◊◊

Think you can design the best roller coaster ever? Would you be brave enough to give it a go? You can do both here, invent your own twisting, turning, gut wrenching extravaganza and then suffer the consequences!

Pirates Of The Caribbean
↔ 0.89m
Rating: ◊◊◊◊

Battle for Buccaneer Gold! With sword in hand, get your crew ready and hop aboard your ship in your quest for pirate treasure. This 5 minute 3-D active waterscape adventure is great fun and so exciting, especially at the end!

Invasion! An ExtraTERRORestrial Alien Encounter
Rating: ◊◊◊

Your mission, if you dare to accept it, is to rescue the earthlings from nasty, evil aliens. Pilot your 4 legged vehicle to victory, it's harder than it looks. Fulfill your mission and get everyone out alive. Great to watch as well as play!

> How do aliens pass the time on long trips?
> They play astronauts and crosses!

↔ Height restriction   ☑ Thrilling ⚡   Spooky   Theatrical
⚡ Noisy   ◆ Wet   Gentle   ♿ Wheelchair access ⊙ Set times

Virtual Jungle Cruise
Grab the family and jump into a real river raft. Take a paddle each and get ready for some raging waters ahead, it's a serious workout! Look out for the dino's, canyons and caves, and prepare for some splashing...

Top Games
Ride The Comix
Rating: ♦♦♦♦
In this 4 minute VR showdown you pull on the mask, grab your light saber and become a 3-D super hero battling evil forces. You can even challenge your mates, it's hilarious!

Games Graveyard
Rating: ♦♦
The grown ups will like it in here - they might even win some of the ancient games like Pacman and Frogger.

Radio Disney SongMaker
Rating: ♦♦♦♦
All Pop Idol wannabees should give this a go! Pick your style (rap, country, pop etc), your lyrics and sing along. If it's up to standard get a copy made (for a cost) and show it off to all of your mates back home!

Virtual Boxing / Snow Boarding / Jet Ski-ing
Rating: ♦♦♦
Show off your sporting prowess on a range of sport themed machines.

BEST OF THE REST

Bumper Cars	Buzz Lightyear's Astroblasters
Adventure Ride	Aladdin's Magic Carpet Ride
Creative Stuff	Animation Academy
	Sid's Create A Toy
	Living Easels
Grub	Cheesecake Factory
Shopping	Emporium
Loos	1st and 5th floors

Hanging Out - Downtown Disney®

Where can you shop, eat, dance, chill, watch a movie, watch some dancing and hang out in the best arcade ever - Downtown Disney! Split into 3 areas, the Marketplace, Pleasure Island (more for grown ups) and the West Side - it is the place to go in the evening.

Top Shows
Cirque Du Soleil®
Rating: ◊◊◊◊

This dazzling circus spectacular is a miraculous feat of acrobatics and will make you go WOW - but so it should 'cos it is really expensive. If you are an arty type and love dance and theatre then it is a huge treat and will really appeal, but if you're not then maybe it's not worth it.

AMC® Pleasure Island 24 Theatres Complex
Rating: ◊◊◊◊

Can you imagine a cinema with 24 different screens - how will you know what to watch with all of the choice? You might have to come back, and back, and back - enough! Anyway not only is it huge it's also kind of cute in an old fashioned way, although it has all the latest gear in terms of sound and vision. Featuring loads of great films from classics to the latest releases, it's a good night out.

Top Shops
World Of Disney
Rating: ◊◊◊

Unbelievable - this is the largest Disney Shop in the whole world. It has everything here you could possibly want, from character costumes

HANDY!
Check out the jewellery room - see if you can identify the hands of the evil villains...

♁ Height restriction   ☑ Thrilling   ⚡ Spooky   ⚟ Theatrical
⚡ Noisy   ◆ Wet   Gentle   ♿ Wheelchair access   ⏱ Set times

to Mickey shaped pasta and mugs, clocks, picture frames - you name it, it's here!

Once Upon A Toy Story
Rating: ♦♦♦♦
Another fantastic shop with every toy imaginable under one roof! The displays alone are worth checking out, including a funky mini Monorail and a mini Sleeping Beauty's Castle. They stock ALL of the Disney's DVDs currently available so come here for anything you can't get in the UK.

LEGO Imagination Centre®
Rating: ♦♦♦♦
Recently done up, this again is one of the best lego shops ever. No matter what kind of lego you like you can find it here, along with some really great lego models - now don't go removing any of the tiles will you?

Top Nosh
Planet Hollywood®
Rating: ♦♦♦♦
Enter the giant blue globe for a star-studded meal of burgers, steak, chicken etc. The menus are really funny - do you recognise any of the stars?

House of Blues®
Rating: ♦♦♦♦
Soul food with soul music, catch the vibe here and get stuck into creole and cajun cooking - nicely spicy!

BEST OF THE REST

Ghirardelli® Soda Fountain and Chocolate Shop
Rainforest Cafe®
Wolfgang Puck® Express
Portobello Yacht Club
Fulton's Crab House

Yum! Yum!

Universal Orlando® Resort

This is a super cool resort, a bit like WDW but smaller, perhaps a bit more grown up, slightly less magical, but just as much fun! With two parks (Universal Studios Florida® and Universal's Islands of Adventure) and a funky entertainment hub (CityWalk) it is ace - if you get to go here as well as WDW it really would be the holiday of a lifetime.

UNIVERSAL ACCLAIM

- Universal Studios Florida®
Access all areas to what claims to be the the number 1 movie and TV based theme park in the whole world, see what you think! Real films are made here, a chance to be a film star maybe? A combination of shows and rides with live action in the streets.

- Universal's Islands of Adventure
This is thrill city. Part designed by and opened by Stephen Spielberg it truly is one of the best parks in the world. Featuring super heros to supersonic rides the only word to describe it is awesome! But beware - it is hardcore so you need to be brave...

- CityWalk®
This happening eating, shopping and general good time complex is free to visit, with free parking after 6pm (although the car park can be a bit of a walk). With the biggest Hard Rock Cafe in the world, a good few other above average restaurants, some cute shops and a 20 screen cinema, what more could you want? This is party central, definitely come for at least one night.

TICK-ET

In general tickets to Universal Orlando Resort are a bit cheaper than WDW tickets.
You can get some special deals on the internet - check out www.universalorlando.com.
You can also buy an inclusive ticket that includes SeaWorld, Busch Gardens (see later) and Wet 'n' Wild.

Hanging Out - Universal Studios

Top Rides
Revenge of the Mummy™

⌖ New York
↻ 1.22m
ⓘ ✍ ✎ eXpress (same as fast-pass)
Rating: ◊◊◊◊

Climb aboard the terror coaster for a frightening frenzy of a ride quite unlike any other. Take care to dodge the fireballs, avoid the sinister scarab beetles and side step the petrifying army of mummies - in fact this one will have you crying for your mummy like you've never done before.

THAT RIDE WAS SO SCARY EVEN MY TONGUE IS SWEATING!!

Why was the mummy so tense? He was all wound up!

Men in Black™ Alien Attack™

⌖ World Expo
↻ 1.07m
ⓘ ✍ ✎ 🧍 eXpress
Rating: ◊◊◊

You are about to enter the 'recruitment programme' for the MIB! Slip on your shades, hop into the attack wagon, take aim and prepare to defeat the nasty evil aliens. Shoot as you screech and swerve to notch up a super high score - are you up to the Will Smith standard?

SUPER SCORE

As you get near the huge alien in Times Square listen up! Zed says push the red button on your control - the 1st person gets a huge 100,000 bonus points...

Back to the Future The Ride®

⌖ World Expo
↻ 1.02m
ⓘ ✍ ✎ ✎ eXpress
Rating: ◊◊◊

From the future to the past and back again in super quick time and without catching your breath! This

69

↻ Height restriction   ✍ Thrilling   ☠ Spooky   Theatrical
✎ Noisy   ● Wet   Gentle   🧍 Wheelchair access   Set times

takes flight simulators to a
new dimension with bangs
and bumps galore as well as
vivid on screen images that'll
have you screaming.   Mind
the dino!!

QUEUE TIP!

Pick up your express
pass for Shrek before
you queue for Jimmy
Neutron (or vice
versa) and hop from
one to the other...

Jimmy Neutron's Nicktoon Blast™

Production Central
1.07m
eXpress
Rating: ♦♦♦

Join boy wonder Jimmy Neutron on a raging rocket
tour of the toon favourites like Rugrats® and
SpongeBob SquarePants®. Everything goes a little-
pear-shaped in the pre-show when Jimmy gets a little
confused when showing off his new spy camera, but it
all leads to fun and games in the end!

E.T. Adventure®

Woody Woodpecker's Kidzone
1.02m (for bikes - anyone can go on a gondola)
eXpress
Rating: ♦♦♦♦

Steven Spielberg helped
create this funky flying
adventure themed on his
film, he even tells you about

What do you call an
overweight ET?
An extra cholesterol!

it at the start. Collect your 'passport' before queuing
in the dark, mysterious wood, setting the scene before
you hop on your magical flying bike. Don't forget to
wish E.T. goodbye, he may have a surprise for you...

JAWS®

San Fransisco / Amity
eXpress
Rating: ♦♦♦♦

Make no mistake, this isn't
just a little pootle around the
lake in a boat. It is a knee-
trembling scare-affair that will
have even the bravest jump

back in fear. It's bad enough when the hungry great white shark appears, but it doesn't stop there! Top notch!

Top Sights, Shows & Parades
Terminator 2: 3D Battle Across Time™

Hollywood

ⓘ 💀 ◄» 🔊 eXpress

Rating: ◊◊◊

Part live action, part 3D film, along with fab special effects - this adventure comes to life right in front of you, quite bizzare but clever. It's really brill when the actors seem to 'fall out' of the fim onto the stage and similarly 'jump' right back into the movie. With an exciting and dramatic story featuring the ace Arnold Schwarzenegger in one of his most famous roles - will you be back?

Twister...Ride It Out®

New York

ⓘ 💀 ◄» 🔊 eXpress

Rating: ◊◊◊

Where do milk-shakes come from? Excited cows!

Your chance to appear right in the middle of this special effects frenzy. First impressions are that you're standing in your bog standard American farmyard, kind of like Dorothy's home in the Wizard of Oz. All very cutesy and all very calm. 'Til the storm begins! Cows will fly, rain will rampage, lightning will slice the sky and you're right in the middle of it! Remember to duck...

DUFF STUFF

- Lucy A Tribute - yaawwnn!
- Woody Woodpecker's Kidzone - mostly kiddie (apart from ET ride), OK for an escape but not for thrill seekers!

Shrek 4-D™

Production Central

ⓘ 💀 ◄» eXpress

Rating: ◊◊◊◊

You've got to see this - you will laugh your socks off! This special Shrek film picks up where the first film ended, with all of the favourite characters Princess Fiona™, Donkey and

ⓞ Height restriction   💀 Thrilling   🔊 Spooky   Theatrical
◄» Noisy   ♦ Wet   Gentle   ♿ Wheelchair access   Set times

of course the lovable ug Shrek®. In this surprising, funny, multi-sensory experience you feel, hear and smell as well as see special effects, good job they don't make you taste too!

Earthquake® The Big One

⌐ San Fransisco / Amity
ⓘ 🚫 🔊 eXpress
Rating: ◊◊◊◊

Another super effects speciality, this time with the earthquake theme. Hold on tight, this really does rock!! It is a bit scary (esp. in the under-ground), but so exciting. You'll also get to find out about the special effects as well as feel them, coo-el.

ARE WE HAVING FUN YET?

What did the ground say to the earthquake? You crack me up!

NICK LIVE!

⌐ Production Central
ⓘ 🕐🔊 eXpress
Rating: ◊◊◊

Your chance to get on TV! Not all shows are televised, but check out the boards at the entrance to see if you will have your 5 minutes of fame. Whatever, you'll have a laugh and have the opportunity to get gunked. Check out the loos here - v. funny!

Universal Horror Make-Up Show

⌐ Hollywood
ⓘ 🕐🔊 🧍 eXpress
Rating: ◊◊◊

Now this is a lot more gruesome that you might expect - only go if you are a blood and gore fan. Discover the revolting secrets of the Make-Up department and some petrifying special effects - truly hysterical in more ways than one! It carries a PG -13 rating (kids under 13 must have their parents permission)...

Top Nosh
International Food and Film Festival
⌨ World Expo
Rating: ♦♦♦

If you're not sure what you'd like to eat go here 'cos there is loads of choice. Whether it's pizza, burgers, chilli or Chinese food that floats your boat you can find it, with healthy options as well as naughty nibs like Ice Cream (yummy!).

GO OUT!
Don't forget you can always nip out to Universal's CityWalk for lunch - the Hard Rock Cafe is especially good. Remember to get your hand stamped!

Lombard's Seafood Grille
⌨ San Francisco/Amity
Rating: ♦♦♦

A dead posh pla(i)ce for fish-fiends! This is probably the nicest eatery in the whole of Universal Orlando®, good for a special ocassion meal. Try lovely fresh lobster and seafood or if you're more of a meat eater get stuck into steak or pasta or even huge sandwiches.

Finnegan's Bar & Grill
⌨ New York
Rating: ♦♦♦

When you've had enough holiday nosh pop down here for some good old fish 'n' chips, bangers 'n' mash or a nice meaty pie! With an Irish theme it's tasty stuff!

SNACK FACTS
Where do you get the best of your faves?

Breakfast	San Fransisco Pastry Co
Burgers	Richter's Burger Company
Hot Dogs	Animal Crackers®
Chips	Monster's Cafe
Pizza / Pasta	Louie's Italian Restaurant
Drinks	Cafe La Bamba
Sweets	Second Hand Rose
Ice Cream	Brody's Ice Cream Shoppe
Milkshake	Mel's Drive In
Puds / Cakes	Beverly Hills Boulangerie

HANGING OUT

♠ Height restriction   ✪ Thrilling ☼ Spooky   ⚘ Theatrical
♪ Noisy   ♦ Wet   ☙ Gentle   ♿ Wheelchair access   ⚐ Set times

Hanging Out - Islands of Adventure

Top Rides
The Amazing Adventures of Spider-Man®

Marvel Super Hero Island®
⋂ 1.02m
ⓘ 🎒 ⚛ eXpress
Rating: ◊◊◊◊

Stroll through the aban-
doned offices of the
Daily Bugle before all hell
breaks loose on the
street, and you are right
in the middle of the may-
hem. A fantastic mix of
ride and 3D film has you
gasping in wonder as

Spidie lands on your car, yelling in fear as Dr Octopus
turns his flaming torch in your direction, and screaming as you plunge over the skyscraper. You won't
believe you haven't travelled an inch - unmissable!

Incredible Hulk Roller Coaster®

Marvel Super Hero Island®
⋂ 1.37m
ⓘ 🎒🎒 eXpress
Rating: ◊◊◊◊◊ (BUT PETRIFYING)

What's big, green, and
sits in the corner all day?
The Incredible Sulk!

Adrenaline Junkies get
their fill on this awesome rip
roaring journey into oblivion. Keep your eyes open if
you dare and don't go straight after lunch or it could
be very messy. What every roller coaster promises to
be but often isn't. Might be a bit of a challenge on the
height front - but absolutely petrifying so don't worry
if you don't make it, just go on Spidey one more time!

Dr Doom's Fearfall®

Marvel Super Hero Island®
⋂ 1.32m
ⓘ 🎒🎒 eXpress
Rating: ◊◊◊◊ (BUT PETRIFYING)

Has Dr Doom got a fright and a half in store for you...

Another one for those with cast iron stomachs. One minute you're zipping up 60m at a rate of noughts, the next you're plummeting earthwards with your stomach in your mouth. The view from the top is great, but who is brave enough to open their eyes? Over before you know it, this is really hard core.

Dudley Do-Right's Ripsaw Falls®
⌐ Toon Lagoon®
∩ 1.12m
① 🎦 ᐞ eXpress
Rating: ⬤⬤⬤

Just another log flume? 'Course not, it is the Islands of Adventure after all! Throwing you through the water comes as a surprise followed by one of the steepest drops ever this will defo. get you wet, wet, wet. There is a story behind it all too, the rescue of lovely Nell, but who cares? It's just about getting wet really!

> **DID YOU KNOW?**
> - This is the first flume ride to go under the water.
> - The logs travel 5m below the water level.
> - The finale is a 25m plunge and max. speed is 45 mph.

Popeye & Bluto's Bilge-Rat Barges®
⌐ Toon Lagoon®
∩ 1.02m
① 🎦 ᐞ eXpress
Rating: ⬤⬤⬤

Save Olive Oyl from the nasty Bluto and get a real soaking in this drenching white water raft ride. Similar to the usual, but somehow bumpier, bouncier and a whole lot wetter. There is no escape so don't try to dodge the deluge. A nice way to cool down!

Jurassic Park River Adventure®
⌐ Jurassic Park®
∩ 1.02m
① 🎦 ᐞ 🧍 eXpress
Rating: ⬤⬤⬤

This is no ordinary raft ride, this river is a dino-fest! Be really careful...some fences are broken and the viscous Raptors have escaped, and the only way out to

∩ Height restriction 🎦 Thrilling Spooky Theatrical
ᐞ Noisy ⬤ Wet Gentle 🧍 Wheelchair access Set times

avoid the hungry jaws of terrifying T-Rex is an 30m drop in dreadful darkness with soaking consequences!

Duelling Dragons®

The Lost Continent®
Ω 1.37m
ⓘ ☣ eXpress
Rating: ▲▲▲

Pick a dragon (fire or ice) and prepare yourself for

Why did the dragon go on a diet ?

He weighed too much for his scales !!

a raging roller coaster race. The queue is entertaining but a pain, just when you think you are there you have to wait for more. Relatively worth it with corkscrews, loops and twists galore and three jaw dropping near misses. Not as good as Hulk though.

Top Sights, Shows & Parades

Jurassic Park Discovery Center®

Jurassic Park®
ⓘ ♟
Rating: ▲▲▲

If you are a dino-fan then get yourself down here. It's an interactive pleasure dome filled with dino facts and exhibits. Best of all is the DNA sequencing tool that lets you make your own prehistoric pal and the raptor hatching vid - educational but entertaining at the same time. Also a cool place to chill out when it's hot!

Poseidon's Fury®

The Lost Continent®
ⓘ ♟
Rating: ▲▲▲

A walk through extravaganza of special effects and dramatic scenes that will make your eyes pop out of your head! Especially amazing is the whopping water vortex tunnel and the final clashing battle scene between the posing Poseidon and the demon Darkennon. It rocks!

The Eighth Voyage of Sinbad® Stunt Show
◄ The Lost Continent®
ⓘ 🎭
Rating: ◊◊◊

Watch super Sinbad rescue the pretty princess Amora amidst explosions and fire in this live-action swash-buckling stunt special.

Top Nosh

Mythos Restaurant®
◄ The Lost Continent®
Rating: ◊◊◊◊

Often voted one of the best theme park restaurants in Orlando, this is funky 'cos of the food and the setting. You're inside a cave in a sleeping volcano with water-falls and fountains; nice and cool too. Serving pizza, pasta and salads the food is usually good. Has a kids menu.

Confisco Grille®
◄ Port of Entry®
Rating: ◊◊◊

A good place for character breakfasts at the weekend, this burger joint also serves yummy snacks the rest of the time. It's the usual stuff, pasta, burgers, salad etc but it is sit down service and tasty enough. Also have a good kids menu and super slushies!

SNACK FACTS

Where do you get the best of your faves?

Burgers	Captain America Diner®
Salads	Circus McGurkus Cafe Stoo-pendous™
Chips	Wimpy's
Pizza / Pasta	Pizza Predattoria
Drinks	Oasis Coolers
Sweets	Cotton Candy
Ice Cream	Hop On Pop™ Ice Cream Shop
Juice	Moose Juice Goose Juice

🎧 Height restriction ☑ Thrilling 🌀 Spooky · Theatrical
🔊 Noisy ◊ Wet Gentle ✦ Wheelchair access ⋆ Set times

Hanging Out - Other Parks

As well as WDW and Universal there are a few other parks to consider... You can get a combined ticket (Orlando Flexticket) that covers the entrance to most of these and to Universal Resort Florida - but leave that to the grown-ups to organise.

SeaWorld® Adventure Park

✉ Central Florida Parkway
☎ (800) 327-2424
ⓘ 9am-7pm off peak,
   9am - 10pm peak
🖳 www.seaworld.com

SEAWORLD UNMISSABLE

- Shamu Stadium - watch the stunning acrobatic Killer Whale extravaganza
- Shark Encounter
- Dolphin Cove - amazing!
- Journey to Atlantis coaster
- Kraken - shocking coaster!
- Nautilus Theater - Odyssea, ace theatrical fantasy show

A fantastic place not to be missed. It's a lot more tranquil than the others yet still has it's fair share of thrill rides, amazing animal exploits and spellbinding shows.

They also host a few special activities like the 'Adventure Express Tour' where you get back door access to rides & shows, the chance to feed animals etc and the super exciting 'Sharks Deep Dive' where

you get right into the Shark Aquarium (in a cage) - but these are at an additional cost and have age and height restrictions.

A real treat is 'Dine with Shamu', when you have dinner 'backstage' with the trainers and the killer whales.

Busch Gardens® Tampa Bay

- ✉ Tampa, 1hr from Orlando via I-4
- ☎ (407) 351-1800
- ① 9.30am-7pm min - call / check websitefor details
- 🖥 www.buschgardens.com

Another amazing place that combines just spine-tingling rides with spectacular wild animals.

With an African theme featuring more than 2,700 creatures of 320 species, it's a zoo and a half. The Rhino Rally safari is cool - not quite up to Animal Kingdom standard but pretty good nevertheless. However the rides are better than AK - there are 7 thrill rides and 3 water rides, the new Sheikra is awesome combining coaster with free fall and a huge splash at the end, completely unmissable. Only drawback is distance from Orlando...

BUSCH G. UNMISSABLE

- Sheikra, the US's first dive coaster, totally wild man!
- Rhino Rally - safari-tastic.
- Gwazi, Kumba, Python & Montu - other fab coasters.
- Akbar's Adventure Tours, an Egyptian simulator adventure!
- Tanganyika Tidal Wave - wet!
- KaTonga - brill show.
- R.L. Stine's 4-D Haunted Lighthouse - clever...

Wet 'n Wild® Orlando

- ✉ International Drive
- ☎ (407) 351-1800
- ① 10am-5pm min - call / check website for details
- 🖥 www.wetnwild.com

With 7 thrill rides, 6 multi-person rides, a kids zone, the Lazy River, a Wave Pool, Volleyball, and a chill-out beach there is something here for everyone, no wonder it's won loads of awards... Best of all is the phenomenal 'Flyer' a four passenger 'bobsled' run, 'Hydra Fighter' the high tech squirt-a-thon and the drain-like 'Black Hole' - truly wild and certainly wet!!

Discovery Cove

✉ Central Florida Parkway
☎ 1-877-4-DISCOVERY
ⓘ 9am-5.30pm
🖳 www.dicoverycove.com

Discovery Cove is like a hidden tropical para-dise, only letting in 1,000 visitors a day. The main reason to come here is to swim with the amazing dol-phins (you have to be over 6); although you can pay a reduced fee just to chill out in the beautiful lagoons.

REASONS TO GO TO D. COVE

If the grown ups aren't sure about splashing out to go to Discovery Cove tell them:

● It's much quieter than the other parks and the oldies need / deserve a rest...

● It seems expensive, but cost includes lunch, snorkel kit, towel, etc and 7 day entrance to SeaWorld across the road.

● You're helping to pay for the conservation and protection of endangered species.

● It's educational - not fun...

Extra special packages include the 'Dolphin Lover's Sleepover' when you get to camp overnight right next to the dolphins and the 'Trainer For A Day' where you get right behind the scenes and learn how to feed and train the amazing animals and birds.

Kennedy Space Center

✉ Cape Canaveral (45 miles)
☎ (321) 449-4444
ⓘ 9am-6pm
🖳 www.kennedyspacecenter.com

Where do astro-nauts leave their space-ships?
At parking meteors!

If you're Space fan then you've just got to go here, it is simply amazing. The Kennedy Space Center tour shows you the awesome NASA facilities, including the mega launch pads, the massive Vehicle Assembly Building and the stunning Apollo/Saturn V Center.

After this check out the live action theatrical show 'Mad Mission to Mars' and get the opportunity to meet a real-live Astronaut, remember to ask him some questions, you won't get this chance again. Explore the full-size Space Shuttle mock-up and watch the IMAX space film on the gigantic screen - excellent! See if any shuttles are launching, you can't miss that.

Hanging Out - Shopping

Some people go to Orlando JUST FOR SHOPPING - can you believe it?! We don't think that you'll be one of them so we're going to cover the best mall (in our opinion) and give you info on the others, hope that's OK with you.

Festival Bay Shopping Mall

✉ Top of I-Drive, Orlando
☎ (407) 351-7718
ⓘ M-Sat 10am-9pm, Sun 12-7pm
🖥 www.belz.com
🖥 www.vans.com/skateparks

This is a shopping centre with a difference 'cos it's got a lots more besides and it is truly top for kids. The highlight has got to be the superb Vans Skatepark, cool just to look at let alone have a go at - check out the website for details. And that's not all - you can even have a go at 'glow in the dark' golf at 'Putting Edge'; go to the cinema (20 screens) or stuff your face full of Rocky Mountain chocolate, Cold Stone Creamery Ice Cream, or yummy burgers from Fuddruckers. Oh yeah, there are loads of shops too!!

SHOP 'TIL YOU DROP

Where do you get the bargains or the funky stuff?

Trainers	Nike & Reebok @ Belz Outlet, I-Drive
Disney Stuff	Downtown Disney
	Character Warehouse, Belz Outlet, I-Drive
Universal Stuff	Universal CityWalk
	Orlando Premium Outlets, btwn I-Drive & I-4
Gap Clothes	Pointe*Orlando, I-Drive
Toys (interactive)	FAO Schwarz, Pointe*Orlando, I-Drive
CD's, DVD's	Florida Mall, South Orange Blossom Trail
V. Posh Gear	Mall at Millenia, I-4 exit 78
Supermarkets	Publix, Goodings & Walmart (huge) on H-192

Hanging Out - Evening Fun!

By the time the evening comes you might be so exhausted that you just want to jump into bed so that you're bright and awake for the next day.

PIZZA-RAMA

At lots of the Disney resort hotels you can have pizza delivered to your room, perfect for a quiet night in!

But just in case your looking for something else to do...

Aside from Universal CityWalk, Downtown Disney and the various shopping malls you can also have fun at one of the special dinner shows. During the day some of them look a bit dodgy from the outside, but when darkness falls they become alive with activity.

EVENING UNMISSABLE

- Downtown Disney
- Universal CityWalk
- Fireworks @ the parks & EPCOT generally
- Shopping (Festival Mall)
- DisneyQuest
- Medieval Times
- Gator Safari At Night

Medieval Times

- ✉ H-192, 6 miles from WDW
- ☎ 1-888-WE-JOUST
- 🖥 www.MedievalTimes.com

Hilarious knight time (tee-hee) jousting and jostling on horseback, set in an old Spanish castle. Boo along with the best of them and get stuck in to your chicken with your fingers - they didn't use cutlery in the old days. Fun!

Gator Safari At Night

- ✉ hotel pick up
- ☎ (407) 522-5911
- 🖥 www.gatortours.com

Expensive but amazing! The bus picks up from you hotel and takes you to the airboat for a ride you will remember. Keep your eyes peeled for the red eyes peering out the water and keep your arms in - don't be gator grub! Fab BBQ too!!

What is worse than an alligator with toothache? A centipede with athlete's foot!

Can't be bothered to read the whole book? Want it all laid out on one page that is easy to follow? Good job we've done these day planners then!

Flexible Friends...

We have included the MUST DO rides and suggested shows/events that will make your days sooper dooper. We can't be exactly precise about what time to do things as times change and you need to be flexible to allow for queueing. Check these out when you arrive in the Parks.

You will need at least one day for each park, more if you want to take your time and chill out taking in the atmosphere. Also you will get tired and a bit parked-out so be prepared to spend some afternoons at your hotel just hanging around by the pool, especially if you've got a big night out planned.

GET IN TOUCH

We'd love to hear your comments about what you think of the Ultimate days, do you agree with them... like to suggest something else...? Then drop us an email at hello@knapsack-guides.com.

Early Doors

On park days start early to fit everything in. Get to the parks in time to queue up as soon as the doors open. If you are staying at a WDW Resort Hotel it is well worth taking advantage of the Extra Magic Hours, your hotel should give you an up to date plan of when these are taking place in each of the 4 main parks.

Go to your favourite ride first thing in the morning and save the other biggies for lunch time (1pm-2pm) and parade time - use Fastpass where poss. Do repeat runs after you've done everything else you want.

We recommend seeing the parades and shows too, they are what Disney is all about!

Day Planner - WDW - MAGIC KINGDOM

PARK: MAGIC KINGDOM		DAYS: Tues / Weds / Fri / Sun	*(italics = extra magic hour)*
	What?	**Where?**	Notes
Extra Magic Hour : Space Mountain, Buzz Lightyear's Space Ranger Spinner, Hanuted Mansion (evening only)			
Morning	Big Thunder Mountain	Frontierland	Explore Tom Sawyer Island whilst you are here
	Pirates of The Caribbean	Adventureland	Then take a look around the Swiss Family's house
	Magic Carpets of Aladdin	Adventureland	
	Jungle Cruise	Adventureland	
LUNCH			
Afternoon	Splash Mountain	Frontierland	
	Liberty Square Riverboat	Frontierland	If you a bit stuck for time have a picnic on the boat
	Mickey's Philarmagic	Fantasyland	Check out Time Guide and fit in
	General scout around Fantasyland	Fantasyland	A bit babyish but sprinkled with lots of fairydust!
	Share A Dream Come True Parade	Main St USA	3pm - but get there 20 mins early for a good spot
	BarnStormer @ Goofy's WiseAcre Farm	Mickey's ToonTown Fair	Chill out wandering around the Toon Town Fair
	Stitch's Great Escape	Tomorrowland	Do it in the afternoon or post evening parade
DINNER / REST			
Evening	SpectroMagic Parade / Wishes	Main St USA	Spectromagic is on most nights - Wishes is only on weekends / special nights. Try to see both!

Day Planner - WDW - EPCOT

PARK: EPCOT

DAYS: Mon / Thurs / Sat / Sun   *(italics = extra magic hour)*

Extra Magic Hour : Mission: SPACE, Test Track (get a FASTPASS for one whilst you go on the other)

	What?	Where?	Notes
Morning	Honey I Shrunk The Audience	Imagination!	Every 20 mins
	Figment / ImageWorks	Imagination!	Only go on Figment Ride if queue is short...
	Living with the Land	The Land	If queue, pick up FASTPASS and come back
	The Living Seas	Living Seas	Come back if you are short on time!
LUNCH			
Afternoon	World Showcase Pavilions	World Showcase Pavilions	Have lunch here, or chill out post picnic!
	Innoventions East & West	Innoventions	Check out future technologies & email your mates!
	Soarin'	Future World	The newest thing in the park!!
	SpaceShip Earth	Future World	It's getting on a bit but still fun!
DINNER / REST			
Evening	Illuminations	World Showcase Lagoon	9pm start but get there an hour ahead
	World Showcase Pavilions	World Showcase Pavilions	Good for dinner or generally hanging out...

85

THE ULTIMATE

Day Planner - WDW - DISNEY - MGM STUDIOS

PARK: DISNEY - MGM STUDIOS	DAYS: *Tues / Weds / Thurs / Sun*	*(italics = extra magic hour)*
What?	**Where?**	**Notes**
Extra Magic Hour : Tower of Terror, Rock 'n' Roller Coaster starring Aerosmith (get a FASTPASS for one whilst you go on the other)		
Morning		
Star Tours	Streets of America	Don't pig out before this, it's a bit rocky...
Jim Henson's Muppet Vision 3D	Streets of America	Continuous 25 min shows, if you've got hang about time check out the 'Honey I Shrunk The Kids' set
Indiana Jones™ Epic Stunt Spectacular	Streets of America	30 minute shows - check Times Guide for exact time
LUNCH : Head on down to the funky Sci-Fi Diner for an early lunch - make sure you book in advance!		
Afternoon		
Disney-MGM Studios Backlot Tour	Mickey Avenue	This is fab - don't miss it! Continuous 35 min tour
Light, Motors, Action!™ Stunt Show	Mickey Avenue	Check Time Guide for show times - be flexible!
Who Wants To Be A Millionaire	Mickey Avenue	Check out Time Guide and fit in with other pm plans.
Magic of Animation	Mickey Avenue	Continuous 20min 'experiences'
Stars & Motor Cars Parade	Hollywood Boulevard	Late pm (4.30 / 5.30) - grab a drink beforehand.
DINNER / REST		
Evening		
Fantasmic!	Hollywood Hills Amphitheater	25 min show - limited capacity so get there in plenty of time, seating starts 2 hours before the show!!

86

Day Planner - WDW - ANIMAL KINGDOM

PARK: ANIMAL KINGDOM		DAYS: *Tues / Weds / Thurs / Sat*	*(italics = extra magic hour)*
	What?	**Where?**	**Notes**
Extra Magic Hour : *(a.m.)* Kilimanjaro Safaris®, Pangani Forest Exploration Trail™ *(p.m.)* DINOSAUR, Primeval Whirl®, TriceraTop Spin			
Morning	Kali River Rapids	Asia	Get a soaking early on - time to dry off!
	Maharajah Jungle Trek®	Asia	Take your time - look out for hidden Mickey's
	Expedition Everest™	Asia	If this is open don't miss out!
	Hop on the little train to Rafiki's Planet Watch to see how the animals are cared for. and discover conservation at it's best!		
LUNCH : Best place in the Rainforest Cafe at the park entrance - it just sooo fits with the surroundings...			
Afternoon	Festival of the Lion King	Camp Minnie Mickey	See Times Guide for Show Times - don't miss!
	It's Tough To Be A Bug®	Discovery Island	Check out the Tree of Life whilst queueing - amazing!
	Discovery Island® Trails	Discovery Island	Take a stroll and enjoy the scenery!
	Jammin' Jungle Parade	Discovery Island	4pm - get a good spotting spot by the lake.
	DINOSAUR	DinoLand USA®	This is scary man - watch the grown ups cower....
	Primeval Whirl®	DinoLand USA®	Hang out in DinoLand USA® until the park closes,
	TriceraTop Spin	DinoLand USA®	there is plenty to get up to and enjoy!
DINNER / REST			
Evening	The animals go to bed early and don't really enjoy fireworks so nighttime is quiet in the Animal Kingdom, so go elsewhere....		
	... and where is better than DisneyQuest!	Downtown Disney	If your ticket doesn't give you access to DisneyQuest then just enjoy Downtown Disney - lots of shops!

THE ULTIMATE

87

Day Planner - UNIVERSAL STUDIOS

PARK: DISNEY - UNIVERSAL STUDIOS

DAYS: Mon / Weds / Fri / Sun

	What?	Where?	Notes
Morning	JAWS	San Francisco / Amity	This one often breaks down - hope it's open for you...
	Earthquake® - The Big One	San Francisco / Amity	Worth queueing for this one...good eXpress option
	Men In Black™ Alien Attack™	World Expo	Single person queue goes quicker if you're brave
	Back To The Future - The Ride®	World Expo	Get your photo taken by the funky car
	E.T. Adventure®	Woody Woodpecker's Kidzone®	
LUNCH : Mel's Drive In is a handy option			
Afternoon	Terminator 2: 3-D Battle Across Time™	Hollywood	
	Universal Horror Make-Up Show	Hollywood	Not for the squeamish...
	Shrek 4D™	Production Central	Get an eXpress pass for this or your Jimmy Neutron
	Jimmy Neutron's Nicktoon Blast™	Production Central	whatever is later to maximise time
	Twister...Ride It Out	New York	
	Revenge Of The Mummy℠	New York	
	Chill out wandering around - so many good photo opportunities!		
DINNER / REST			
Evening	Hang Out at Universal CityWalk - Hard Rock Cafe maybe?		

88

Day Planner - Universal's Islands Of Adventure

PARK: DISNEY - Universal's Islands Of Adventure		DAYS: Mon / Tues / Thurs / Fri	
	What?	Where?	Notes
Morning	Incredible Hulk Coaster®	Marvel Super Hero Island®	Note height restrictions on these two - if you're not
	Doctor Doom's Fearfall®	Marvel Super Hero Island®	tall enough move on to Spidies ace ride!
	The Amazing Adventures of Spider-man®	Marvel Super Hero Island®	SUPERB!
	Dudley Do-Rights Ripsaw Falls®	Toon Lagoon®	Two wet ones, best when the sun shines so that you
	Popeye and Bluto's Bilge-Rat Barges®	Toon Lagoon®	dry off quicker!
LUNCH : Mythos in the Lost Continent is a real treat...			
Afternoon	Jurassic Park River Adventure®	Jurassic Park®	Nice after lunch cruise...
	Jurassic Park Discovery Center®	Jurassic Park®	Educational but fun - honest!
	Pteranodon Flyers®	Jurassic Park®	Great views!
	Eighth Voyage Of Sinbad® Stunt Show	The Lost Continent®	Time for a sit down...
	Duelling Dragons®	The Lost Continent®	Fire or Ice - you choose...
	Poseidon's Fury®	The Lost Continent®	Temple Tour of surprises...
	The Cat In The Hat™	Seuss Landing®	More fun than thrilling!
DINNER / REST			
Evening	Hang Out at Universal CityWalk - catch a movie perhaps?		

89

HANDY STUFF

Childline – free 24hr   0800 1111
NSPCC Child Protection Helpline 0808 800 5000

Emergencies
Police / Ambulance / Fire   911
Tourist Oriented Policing Service (TOPS) - I-Drive, Orlando

British Vice-Consulate Orlando
⌐ Suite 2110, Sun Trust Center, 200 South Orange Avenue
Orlando, FL 32801
☎ +1 407-581-1540
⌐ www.britainusa.com/orlando/

Disney® Information
⌐ www.waltdisneyworld.com
Walt Disney World® Resort Guest Relations
☎ +1 407-939-6244
⌐ email: use the 'Contact Us' section at the bottom of the home page on the website
⌐ www.wdisneyw.co.uk
⌐ www.guide2wdw.com
⌐ http://allearsnet.com/
⌐ www.intercot.com
⌐ www.themeparkinsider.com

Universal® Information
⌐ www.universalorlando.com
Universal Orlando® Resort Guest Relations
⌐ 1000 Universal Studios Plaza, Orlando, Florida 32819-7610
☎ +1 407-224-4233
⌐ www.themeparkinsider.com
⌐ www.themeparks.com/unifl/

Don't forget to get lots of brochures from your local travel agents, they tell you what they think of the place and you'll see lots of photos. The 'Funway Holidays' one is very good!

Celebrations
- Get your free birthday badge at City Hall in the Magic Kingdom and at Guests Services in the other parks.
- Order birthday cakes when you check in to your hotel.
- Tell every cast member you meet that it's your birthday to get extra special service!

Cash Points (handy places to take your parents...)
- At the entrance of each of the WDW parks plus...
- By the Liberty Tree Tavern in the Magic Kingdom®
- At the corner of Innoventions West In Epcot®
- By the Toy Story Pizza Planet in Disney-MGM Studios
- Just before the Port of Entry at Universal's Islands of Adventure and by the Lost Continent toilets in the park!
- To the right of the Front Lot in Universal Studios Park and next to the toilets on Rodeo Drive
- At the Gaumont Cineplex in Disney® Village.
- At the Convention Centre in Disney's Newport Bay Club.

Postcards
Mailing postcards is <u>so</u> yesterday - email them instead. Epcot has a couple of places where you can send funky e-cards, just remember to take a list of your mates email addresses and sign up to a mobile email account.

Tourist Information
Visitors Center Official, 8723 International Dr, Orlando, FL 32819
☎ +1 407-363-5872

Pick up leaflets, magazines and discount voucher booklets from hotel entrances, restaurant foyers or ticket booths in shopping centres and main streets.

- www.orlandotouristinformationbureau.com
- www.visitflorida.com
- www.go2orlando.com
- www.orlandoinfo.com

Transport
Public transport for Orlando.
- www.golynx.com
- www.iridetrolley.com

General Fun Websites
- www.lego.com
- www.discovery-kids.co.uk
- www.kidstravelfun.com

FINALLY BUT MOST IMPORTANTLY!!!
- www.knapsackguides.com
- Knapsack Publishing Ltd., The Beach Hut, PO Box 124, Hove. BN3 3JP
☎ 01273 737276